The Devil Within

The Story of Recovering a Lost Voice

by

Angela Caine

VoiceGym
Southampton
www.voicegym.co.uk

First edition, published September 2006

by

VoiceGym
436 Winchester Road, Southampton SO16 7DH, U.K.
www.voicegym.co.uk

ISBN-13: 978-0-9553799-4-9
ISBN-10: 0-9553799-4-6

Printed by Zap Digital Print Ltd
Woodbridge Meadows, Guildford GU1 1BA, U.K.
www.zaprepro.co.uk

In Memory of Judy

Acknowledgements

It is difficult to think of one person in my life that has not in some way contributed to this book. We are so much the result of our relationships, both close and transitory, because without them we have little to respond to and the measure of us is in those responses.

My parents made my childhood what it was and it was both challenging and wonderful. What a pity I never told them, but then I never knew. My schools – Middleton Schools Nottingham, Christ Church Primary School Rhyl and Rhyl Grammar School, were memorable for the teachers that guided, praised and scolded me. Of my music teachers Leslie Murchie taught me how to play the piano and much more and Walther Gruner introduced me to German Song. Fellow student Enid Hartle shared various lodgings and gave me the Northern vowels that I have had ever since.

My family and other personal relationships do not appear directly because this is a book about losing my voice and its recovery. However I do recognise the hurt that my erratic and often incomprehensible behaviour brought them. I hope they will accept that this book is to prevent it ever happening to anyone again and the need for the story to be told. Alexander Evans, now a professional singer, allowed me to tell his personal story of voice loss through premolar extraction and other singers have allowed me to present films of their struggles with voice problems in spite of the admission of problems not being good for the singer's 'professional image'.

I had two very strict editors. Dr Jackie Porter, MD., a retired General Practitioner and friend, who has canoed white water and believes in patient responsibility, helped me to edit forty years of collected writing, much of it too angry and hurt to make any sense. She calmed the anger and extracted the sense from it. Andre Hedger BDS, LDS., RCS.Eng., FHS., FRGS., a colleague, friend and serious mountain climber corrected dental technicalities and made sure that the connections between voice and dental treatment were clear. My husband Chris appears in the book because he played a major part in my recovery; taught me how to present my work and then supported its publication … and everything else about me.

Angela Caine, 2006

Contents

Chapter 1: The Wizard

Our birth is but a sleep and a forgetting,
The star that rises with us, our life Star
Has had elsewhere its setting
And cometh from afar.
Not in entire forgetfulness,
And not in utter nakedness
Do we come…

William Wordsworth

I keep piecing the story together and just when I feel I have the explanation clear in my head, something else happens to bring back another memory that changes everything and I'm back groping about. I had thought it all began with my birth and my mother and I now have the story clear from then, but where did the music come from? No-one else in a family that more resembles a tribe was there another musician, so why suddenly a child that played the piano at four and for whom the voice and singing was a life force. Perhaps I'm not going back far enough. Maybe I have to begin *before* my birth and before she was my mother, when she was a widow with two small boys and no thought of me or the possibility of me. I will start again and go all the way back to the wizard and see if that makes the final difference. Because at the time of the wizard she was not my mother I will call her Maud.

Maud lived with her husband and two young sons in rented accommodation at the seaside. The family had moved there for the man to fulfil a contract installing electricity in rows of terraced houses. The great flu epidemic of 1930 killed a thousand people in the first week He was a fit working man on the Friday and died on the Sunday. Maud had no widow's pension, he was not paid up. No provision at all had been made for her and the boys in the event of such a personal disaster and it was clear that unless money could be found the family may yet be divided some more. The Catholic Church offered to take the boys and bring them up in whichever of their boarding schools had room, but that might be anywhere so the woman refused. Her one possibility of rescue was that unlike most women in 1930 she had a professional training. She was a confectioner.

When she was sixteen Maud had fought hard and long with her father to move from the sleepy East Yorkshire market town where he was a successful butcher, killing his own beast, making his own sausages, chitterlings, pies and meat puddings. He supplied the local workhouse till it closed and had more than enough employment for his four daughters. The second daughter did not see this as providing a springboard for the ideas she was developing from the abundance of books at the local village school. She read all the books the girls were allowed to read- classics of literature, manuals of handwork and poetry. She won the poetry prize, not for writing it, but for being able to recite the most poems from memory.

She was finally allowed to go to the nearest big town to work because a relative had a bakery and cake shop and would 'keep an eye on her'. She progressed so well making bread and cakes that she was offered an apprenticeship in one of the grand confectioners of the North – Sissons of Southport. Her transition from local village butcher's daughter to the elegance and pleasure seeking of the Northern Wealthy took a mere two years. Her apprenticeship lasted three years and then she was appointed Head of 'fancy cakes' because of her flair for all things decorative. She was now 21 and allowed to live out of the shop and in her own accommodation. But her head was still full of poetry and Jane Eyre and she was not a bit street wise.

Grandfather butcher and his shop

The tall, dark, suave and handsome man had no trouble at

all. She was captivated by the attention and sophistication. No boys at home had ever been like this, playing golf and billiards and wearing fashionable suits. He was contracted to install electric lighting into houses built for gas, and generally stayed in one place about two years. Before the Southport contract was completed his attractive confectioner was pregnant. He came from a long line of responsible Catholics so they were married and moved together to Middlesborough. There they lived in rented accommodation and he played golf and snooker at the local Conservative club. 13 months after the first son was born, Maude had her second boy.

It is difficult to get a flavour of this marriage. Even the sons, when grownup, could not throw light on the relationship, for they were six and seven when father died and when the woman became my mother she did not speak of this time and neither did her sisters; my aunts.

First it was Middlesbrough, then Leeds, then Rhyl and an apartment overlooking the sea, rented from a wealthy furniture maker. The boys, now five and six, were enrolled in the local Catholic School. The furniture maker's business was in Nottingham but he had thirteen children of his own, now grown up, and all working for the family business. He had begun his property speculation in Rhyl by buying a boarding house on the new railway line to Holyhead so that the whole extended family could spend the summers at the sea, presided over and fed by the central matriarch, his wife of some fifty years. With a nose for making money and seeing the way things were going in the holiday business he purchased another five houses on the promenade where you could rent an apartment by the sea. It was in such an

The furniture maker and his shop

apartment taken on a long term let that the new widow found herself with nothing in the world and apparently nowhere to go but home to her father the butcher, where her sisters would help her bring up the boys. The offer of a boarding school place from the Catholic Church was never a serious consideration. She knew that road meant giving them up so she stepped out of her husband's church for ever.

The furniture maker came to the rescue, or was it grandma-furniture- maker? Maud could have the apartment over looking the sea for as long as she needed it rent-free. It would now be possible for her to keep the boys if she could only find a job that would pay living expenses. There was an advertisement for a master baker 11 miles away along the coast. With her experience she got it easily although bread was not her speciality and the hours were difficult. 6am to 3pm daily, Saturdays 6am to10.30am, closing at lunchtime. She could easily be home for the boys out of school at 4pm, but how would she do 6am? There was not a train to get her there so she would have to cycle. The furniture maker's family offered to take care of the boys in the morning. Two children more or less were no problem and she could then leave at 4.30 am to be at work for 6. At 3.30 pm, work over, she could put her bike in the guards van and come home on the train.

A year later a position of head confectioner became vacant in Rhyl and her ordeal was over but she had never missed a day and kept her boys. The boys went to family in Yorkshire for holidays and they all went for Christmas. Once a fortnight her sister sent her a parcel of meat and wrote on it, 'Keep in a Cool Place' for the benefit of the post office. It was now 1934, she was well paid and, with the boys getting older, life was easier. She began to enjoy herself again. She offered to pay rent but the furniture maker said,

The furniture maker and his wife

"Put it in the Post Office for the boys. I don't need it"

Friends who had a car took her to Aintree for the Grand National. She pawned a pair of ugly candlesticks, a gift from family, to pay for a flutter on the horses and won. She bought all new linen sheets for home and with the money over bought herself a dress and matching hat. It was the first money she had spent on herself since she was single. It gave her new life. Friends went with her to the theatre to show off the new dress and hat.

It was a variety show. The top of the bill was a fortune-teller. He sent an assistant into the audience to ask a volunteer to hold up an article and name it. The fortune-teller then described past events in which both article and owner had been involved. He then went on to predict future events in their lives. It was not difficult to work out the system. There are many common events and predictions to everyone's life; it merely took a good show-man to turn them into wizardry. Looking for the next volunteer the assistant was attracted by the hat. Maud decided to have a bit of fun with him and felt in her purse for the wedding ring she had taken off to work with cake mixture.

"A wedding ring from a lovely lady in a striking hat" said the assistant.

There was a pause, the first hesitation in his demonstration.

"It is your ring but you are not currently married, I do not see a man. I see children, maybe two or three, definitely not one"

There was another long pause and the audience was silent and still.

"You will be married again though, and you will have a daughter. She will be famous. There is something else. We must wait for it to come into my mind".

He made a sweeping, dramatic gesture with both arms to call down this 'message'. There had not been such suspense in the Queen's Theatre Rhyl since the psychological thriller 'Gaslight' rocked the town. He lowered his arms and gestured to the woman.

"Your daughter will be a famous musician".

After the performance Maud and friends went to the Queen's bar, where they laughed off the whole episode. Who was going to marry a woman of 35 with two children?

"It was the hat. He couldn't see how old you were"

"Another baby? No thank you. I'm just beginning to have a life, anyway I'm too old. If he can see this in my life then he's not a fortune-teller, he's a wizard".

Still it did leave just a small flutter in her stomach. The event had not been totally dismissed. So when the furniture maker took Maud aside one Saturday afternoon and suggested that she should marry his youngest and unmarried son she was not quite as speechless, shocked or indignant as she expected to be.

"What are you going to do when I am not here? You will lose your home and all that goes with it. You are part of my family and I would like to make sure you still have that security when I am dead and gone. My youngest son adores you, you must have noticed"

She hadn't. In fact she had hardly noticed him at all except to show gratitude when he drove her places; to work sometimes when she was late. He worked as an upholsterer in the business. All the eleven sons and two daughters were trained in the different skills needed for the business of furniture making, but the youngest, who was now 38 had wanted to be an engineer. When he was taken from school at twelve and apprenticed he satisfied this longing by also servicing his father's cars and lorries, meanwhile owning a motorbike and sidecar and his pride and joy, a wooden speed boat with inboard engine.

Then the furniture maker said something very attractive.

"When I die the estate will be divided up. All the children will get a piece of it and they will all be quite well off. You don't want to work all your life and it will be security for the boys. You don't want to miss out on that after being part the family for all these years. He's shy. You'll have to give him a push."

When Christmas came the journey had to be made up into the welsh hills to collect the turkeys all the married children were given for a Christmas present. Sending the unmarried son was supposed to make this

Family Outing

annual gift a surprise. Maud discovered when he was going and offered to go for company. She put on her prettiest dress.

"You look nice"

She knew him for a man of few words, but she had plenty and to spare. When they had picked up the turkeys she suggested they stop at the brow of the hill and look down to see the lights of Rhyl in the distance. She snuggled nearer and he kissed her. He was clumsy and embarrassed but he said,

"I've always loved you but I didn't think you'd want me. Your hands are always so nice. Look at mine."

He spread his thick, stubby fingers in the moonlight, short nails, grimed from car engines and upholsterer's glue. He stared at th distant lights to say

"I'd marry you, you know, if you were willing"

"Yes, I'm willing"

"Are we engaged then?"

"I suppose so"

It was as if those few words had unlocked a flood. He chatted and planned and promised all the way home and she was the one of few words, wondering what she had done. Well, it was done and as his father said, it would secure her future. The boys were delighted, he was the only man they knew who had a car, a motorbike and a boat. The family were also delighted, they had all thought for a long time that he ought to be married and settled down. The next week he asked for measurements for suits to be made for the boys with jackets, caps and long and short trousers. He brought her a tray of rings and of course she picked the biggest and best. Much later in their life together he told her that the rings came from a pawnbroker friend and were a selection of new and second hand. The big one she chose was an unredeemed pawn and cost £15. The new ones were more expensive. She would always hold it against him even though she could not fault the ring she chose.

"You got a second hand wife and gave her a second hand ring. I should have known everything would be second hand from then on".

"I have a nose for a bargain – like my father".

The furniture maker died during their engagement and as he predicted, it was the beginning of selling off the houses and the cars. The business was left to the children to carry on or sell. In his last days he made the couple promise to go ahead with the wedding plans to marry the following Christmas and only when his estate was finally wound up after the wedding did the woman discover who was looking after whom. The patriarch had made provision for his youngest and most vulnerable son by marrying him to a woman who could work hard and bring in the money, because he had none to leave and the business was failing fast through lack of investment and modernisation. Soon her husband would likely be unemployed.

In the face of this and the impending conflict with Germany, policies were changed to keep the business alive and feed the eleven families living from making furniture. Handmade and carved gave way to utility furniture and kitting out barracks with cheap plywood cabinets for an expanding military force

After Maud was married the apartment overlooking the sea was swapped for a narrow rented three storey terraced house on a main road in Nottingham with a blue brick yard at the back and a shop at the front. The trams ran in front and Players factory was across the road offering opportunity to sell fresh baked bread and cakes, sandwiches and pies to complete the household budget. The boys went to local schools and Maud once again set about earning her living.

When one morning, a year after opening the shop, she realised that she had missed a period Maud took off her apron and went into the yard.

"You're thirty nine and you're going to have a baby. Everyone laughed and said it wasn't possible".

She no longer thought of him as a fortune–teller. He was now truly a wizard. She laid her face on the cool wall.

"I don't want it. I don't want to start again. I'm doing my bit. We're getting along. He's kind and good to the boys, funny even, and fun. But a new baby is different. It's a different level of being together and there'll be thirteen years between her and the boys. Her? Well Yes. It'll be a girl and she'll be a musician. There's that responsibility. Money for that"

The smell of baking drifted into the yard and she went in to save the cakes...

There wasn't much choice but to work right through the pregnancy. He helped and the boys helped. All three were so excited about the new baby. He had never thought in his wildest dreams that his embarrassed fumbling would produce a child, but now he was ecstatic. The boys had no idea what a baby would bring but preparations caused so much to-ing and fro-ing of friends and relatives, so much fuss and attention that it must be good.

At the eleventh hour Maud wrote the announcement cards, bought pink for a girl. The concern of the midwife that it had been thirteen years since her previous baby and the rising mortality figures with the age of the mother was shrugged off. She knew she would have this baby and it would live. How could it be a musician if it did not live?

At five thirty on the 7th May she shut the shop and cleared the window. She cashed up, out of breath with walking back and forth from the back room, wrapping up yesterday's loaves to sell cheap in the morning. The boys were out at their clubs, the ATC and the Boxing Gym and she sat down, exhausted and holding herself to relieve the weight hanging from her middle.

When the pain came she was shocked. There had been so much conjecture, so much talk of what this baby would be, what it would do. She had always seen it lying in its cot, the youngest and most beautiful baby in this great tribe of a family that she was beginning to resent for their intrusion and interference. She had pictured a tall, elegant girl in a long frock sitting playing the shiny piano while she looked on proud and smug. She had not thought through how the baby would get out of her and into the cot. She had avoided thinking of the pain of it. Now she didn't want that and she began to hold herself tight and cry.

He found her, legs doubled underneath, in the corner of the settee in the back room when he came from work. He came from a big family, babies were born all the time but he never saw it. It was whispered about by the women and then the baby was there. They had never talked about the birth, only about after. The cot he had made lovingly at work stood upstairs. In it was the first nightdress, a terry towelling square and rubber knickers, Blankets cut down to size and bound each cut end with pink ribbon were ready to wrap the new baby. All was ready in the little room with the sloping ceiling, distempered with a little drop of cochineal from the cake colouring to turn it pink. This seemed all wrong, not in the plan. The women in the family had offered to be here for this moment so she would not be alone, but she refused saying she would be alright, she had had two babies already. Why didn't she allow them to help? She was now howling and appeared to be losing control of herself.

"Is this the baby coming? Tell me what to do. I can look after you if you just tell me what to do".

He took her hands and she calmed down. When the pain went she could think, but she was terrified of the pain. He got her up the narrow stairs by putting his shoulder under her bum and lifting her every step. He thought they had never done anything as intimate before as together getting her up those stairs. Maybe the baby could be a beginning. When she was laid down the pain came again and she clung to him in terror, trembling and teeth chattering... Downstairs a door opened and shut.

"I must go and send the boys down the road to sleep. Then I must go for the midwife".

The boys wanted to come up. Had she got their sister yet? How long would it be? She was hysterical and he couldn't let them see her. Arrangements had been made for the boys to go to family down the road. He had to take them; he couldn't expect them to report this. When he left them his sister-in-law wanted to come back with him but he daren't cross his wife and said she would rather do it herself. Well she would. She insisted. The boys said they wouldn't go to sleep and must be fetched straight away the baby was born. He promised and left to go back and check his wife before cycling the mile or so for the midwife. There was no sound on the stairs and in the bedroom, her eyes were closed. The bed was wet and bloody, her fingers wound tight around the pillows. She showed no sign of life and he was terrified. He fled on his bike for the midwife.

When he returned to the house she was making noises that hit him in the pit of his stomach so he did not go upstairs with the midwife but buried himself in the corner of the settee with a cushion over his head. He did not know this wife.

Maud had been alone for an hour and the midwife found the baby's head presenting and the cord around its neck. The midwife stopped the woman's frantic desire to rid her system of this baby by briskly telling her to

"Stop your noise. We can't think here and you're doing yourself no good. You'll lose this baby if you go on like this".

My father was brought out from under his cushion to fetch the doctor while the midwife did her best to gain my mother's confidence with a continual flow of calm and reason.

My mother calmed until the doctor arrived and she realised that she would have to be cut to save the baby. She clambered up the bed, holding on to the bed rails and kicking out in spite of her pain until the doctor and the midwife dragged her back by the legs and while the midwife held them, the doctor cut a space for the baby's head and pulled it out. The baby's face was going blue when the cord snapped at its attachment in the navel and the girl was free of her mother. They showed her the baby to reassure her that it was alright but the woman wanted none of it. The doctor stitched the woman who was now in shock and they cleaned her up. The girl was born at 3 am.

The midwife took the little girl downstairs and gave her into her father's arms. Her mother slept in the bed and the man watched the baby sleep between cushions on the settee. Before the midwife left at 5 am they both cleaned the baby and he watched her dress his little girl in her terry towel nappy, rubber pants and nightdress. She then gave him the baby and he put her gently into her cot and covered her with the pink edged blanket.

She slept all the while, as if all she needed was to be left alone, but he could not sleep, so he watched her until the boys came home at 9am.

They brought an armful of bluebells for the baby but settled for putting one on her pillow for when she woke up. The woman was recovered, bright and welcoming. She wanted to see her new daughter and the baby, as if summoned, cried to be fed. The new family gathered, the woman proud and smiling with the baby in her arms, sons on either side stroking the new little girl and chattering, father at the foot of the bed looking on.

From the first she was what her mother called 'forward'. She did not seem to need to be a baby in a pram, never bothered to crawl and with two such older brothers to encourage her on to her feet she soon chattered and sang, toddling in and out of the shop with independence beyond any expectations.

When she was two the war forced them out of the city. The boys were old enough to volunteer to fight and after the war they married and had their own homes. The household became three and she became an only child with lots of time alone. The shop was no longer needed and for the first time Maud did not have to work. They rented a house on the edge of the city and built an Anderson shelter in the garden. They bought a black ebonised upright piano for when the girl was ready to play it.

Now the woman could spend time working on her dream. She drew and painted with her little daughter; they sang songs and Maud recited to her the poems she had learnt as a girl while they went walks to collect blackberries, nuts, or flowers. They danced in the kitchen waiting for cakes in the oven. The woman still made birthday and wedding cakes as long as the ingredients came with the order. People still got married in spite of the war, were christened and had birthdays, so butter and sugar was saved for the occasion.

The little girl danced with her mother and clapped her hands to the rhythm. She climbed onto the big piano stool and thumped up and down the black and white notes. Her mother had played as a girl and helped her to pick out tunes. When the girl was four and could play all the tunes her mother decided it was time to begin in earnest. There was a school of music in the city, a distance of about six miles. Children were taken 'on approval'. They had three lessons and if they took to it they could stay. Lessons for school age children began at 4 pm, Monday to Friday, but the early slots were already taken... 7.30pm was the first time available.

Appointments were made. The lessons were on Thursdays and it was pointed out most strongly that lessons must not be missed for any but the most serious of reasons. Father was on air raid duty on Thursdays so it was left to mother to provide the transport. A seat was made for the back of mother's bike. Two cycle lamps, one red one clear, were fitted with metal slotted covers to keep the light directed on the road. You did not show lights that could be seen from above. Nottingham is a hilly city and the family lived downhill from the centre. That meant six miles uphill with a four year old on the back. Mother cycled every week in school term time summer and winter the six miles up hill, relieved by freewheeling down again. During the lesson she waited in the cemetery across the way, sitting on a bench under the trees, thinking of the wizard and satisfied that the prophecy was being fulfilled.

Chapter 2: The Coming of the Angel

I was about five when I had my first two wheeler. Bikes were scarce in 1942 and the one that turned up was a boy's bike a size too big. I could ride the bike once I was on but it was so hard to get on and off because of the bar between saddle and handlebars. When my dad first lifted me on I couldn't reach the pedals so he put wooden blocks on them and then I could reach. But to get my leg over the saddle I had to lift my skirt with one hand. Skirts were obligatory for little girls. That hand couldn't hold onto the bike. At first I rode the bike when my dad came home from work. He put me on, gave me a push and I rode around the road that encircled the houses on our block. There was no traffic except the odd bike, maybe one car. There was no petrol for private motoring. I had a bell and as I approached our house I rang it furiously, but generally my dad was in the shed or in the house with the radio on and I had to go round again. Sometimes he would come out just in time to see me disappear round the corner and go in again. I had to have an alternative and not rely on anyone.

Instead of ringing my bell I pulled on my brake and ran sideways against the low front garden wall hoping to stop with my bike leaning against the wall. Instead it leaned the other way and off I came. Realising I was not hurt but just frightened I set out to modify my plan. Getting on was easier. Leg over from crouching on the top of the wall meant I could hold up my skirt with one hand and the bike with the other while I located the pedal with one foot. A good push off with the land foot and I was away.

Getting off never got any better until I tucked my dress in my knickers and got off like I saw the boy down the road get off. But in the meantime I discovered that when I fell off the best thing to do was go and play the piano. Something happened when I played the piano. It was as if someone stroked my hair and kissed me and took the pain away. The night of the air raid this someone became my angel. When the sirens went we slept in the shelter in the garden. The nearby anti-aircraft guns that pounded and bent the leaded windows of the house meant nothing to me. They were not in my world, which was safe and happy and forever interesting. Raids and guns were only at night, muffled by the earth and grass on top of the shelter as we slept..

But this night it was decided that I should see the glow in the sky as Boots factory and the Co-op took direct hits and the pharmaceuticals from the one and the butter and oils from the other lit the night sky. The sky was so clear and above us the stars twinkled and shone. Always ready with a story my mother painted the picture of the heaven sprinkled with the lights the angels carried as they went about looking after people.

"...and you needn't be frightened of the bombs because your angel will shelter you with great big wings and take all your hurt away, like this... "

...and I was bundled tight in her arms and snuggled back in my bunk bed in the shelter.

So that is how my angel became my comforter when I was hurt and the staunch support and critic of my piano playing. I no longer sat in the front room playing the piano alone. Someone always watched and listened. Someone was always pleased with what I did, even when I couldn't find my way through the music and made so many mistakes. There was a hand on my shoulder encouraging me to stay there, wait a while, play something else I knew to clear my head and give my brain a chance to think about the new stuff. My angel taught me how to enjoy my music for myself. When I was trotted out at parties and family occasions and my mother was unable to contain her delight and pride at 'her prodigy' I played for myself and for the angel and then wanted only to slip away to bed. Tucked up we would go over it together, enjoying the excitement of the moments when fingers did just what they were expected to do, knowing that we were in a different world from the people who were the audience.

I was still only about six when The School of Music held a public concert in Nottingham's Albert Hall. I was told to play two pieces out of the book of five that were my special favourites. Mother made me a yellow silk dress and there were new shoes, new socks and hair ribbon. There was a new feel about this occasion, a sort of crawling sensation in the bottom of my stomach. Mother seemed very edgy and snapped about not sitting down on the bus so I wouldn't crease. The hall was very big and the piano quite the wrong shape but I knew now that I would get help whatever happened so up I went and someone hitched me onto a cushion on the stool and put my music up for me. The piano was like a live thing. It made so much noise and I could see my hands playing twice, once on the piano and backwards in the shiny lid. By the time I had thought about all this I had played two pieces but it was so wonderful playing that huge piano that I played all five pieces and then the audience clapped for ages and I did not know what to do next, so I got off the stool and stood there. The Head of the School came up on the stage, took my hand and led me off.

"Well done dear", she said "But I thought you were up there for the night".

Gradually, through six, seven, eight and nine, I spent more and more of my time playing the piano. I began to escape into it when other things and other people were boring, or when I was hurt. I soon realised that I could also avoid tasks, responsibilities and punishment. If I could just get to the piano before it happened: before I was asked: before I was caught and begin to play, the pursuer would stop, listen and go quietly away, leaving the door open. I would then play until I decided the problem had melted away. My music was now my comforter and side step to life. I never considered how much it meant to me any more than I considered my parents, my breathing, school or any other fundamental. They were just there. I was part of them and they were part of me. It was simple.

When I was eight the war ended, grandma died and the family furniture business finally closed for ever. From the final sale of the property my father inherited £1,500.00. Both of my parents were forty-eight. Something had to be done that would stretch the money into a property to live in – our house was rented and the lease had ended – and employment for my father that would raise a pension in approximately another fifteen years. For about a month I was sent to bed early, where I lay and listened to unfamiliar agitated conversation downstairs and then I was told we were moving to Rhyl. The money had been used to purchase the remaining one of grandfather's old boarding houses, the one where my grandmother had lived and presided over the family holidays. We became purveyors of Board Residence and Bed and Breakfast and my dad got his first commercial garage and his first very own car.

The house was a monument to my grandfather, containing his furniture and preserved by my grandmother. It missed the war by being requisitioned by the army for officer's quarters but then never used. From a 1930s detached house with a tiled bathroom we stepped back into Victorian living.

The house was on five floors, four rooms to a floor. It had no plumbed hot water and above the ground floor there was one cold water tap on each floor in a deep square sink in what had been a linen room. This was a windowless large cupboard off each landing housing the service lift that carried everything needed from the basement stores. The ground floor housed kitchens, pantries and storerooms. The first floor had been my grandmother's apartment, with two lounges filled with monumental Victorian furniture over looking the sea and two bedrooms at the back similarly furnished. The upper three floors were each divided into two apartments, each apartment having a back room and a front room. The front room had a large velvet three piece suite in the bay window overlooking the sea, two double beds, a double wardrobe and matching dressing table, a large marble fireplace with shelved over-mantle for nick-knacks and a marble-topped wash stand with a complete set of patterned china for washing. On the wall was a bell pull to summon staff to bring hot water, early morning tea and meals via the service lift. The back room was altogether less well appointed with a double bed, wardrobe, dressing table and wash stand with a plain china washing set. Where the front room had a carpet, the back room had only lino and no bell. The back room was for the children of the family and possibly a maid.

The house in Rhyl

On each floor there was a toilet but no bathroom anywhere. Baths were taken in a portable tub in front of the kitchen fire, so had to be planned. Hot water was obtained from a tap on the huge solid fuel black range in the kitchen, which had to be constantly fed and then banked up at night and damped to keep it 'ticking over', unless the wind changed direction, when it went out. Then there was only cold to wash in. The range water tank was filled every morning and a timetable of filling had to be strictly adhered to lest an empty tank explode with the heat of the fire and blow the house and everyone in it to kingdom come.

The house could be purchased cheaply from the estate because it came with conditions. Although my grandmother had died, her two spinster sisters, now in their eighties, had not. They had been taken into our house by my grandfather on retirement from nursing psychiatric patients. In Victorian times this amounted to living in a closed lunatic asylum and looking after the inmates. One condition was that these old ladies should be allowed to live out the rest of their probably fairly short lives in their own home. They lived in one room on the first floor, rarely went out and appeared only at mealtimes. They wore long clothes with beads and pearls, had tight grey curls all over their heads and gave my mother the most amazing underclothes to wash. They showed me how they made their tight curls and how I could make ringlets by twisting pieces of hair around strips of paper and knotting the ends. I once saw them ready for bed with their heads wrapped in paper 'bumble bees' and imagined them sitting up straight in bed asleep, unable to lie on these bees. I decided then and there I must never get old.

When I was ten I caught head lice in my long blond hair. My mother, terrified and ashamed of her dirty daughter did not know what to do and prepared to cut my hair short. The great aunts knew exactly what to do. They seized me, sat me in the kitchen and hung my head over a large newspaper. While one rubbed paraffin through my hair the other combed it with a wooden comb. Little creatures and eggs, coughing and choking on the paraffin fell out of my hair and onto the newspaper. After about an hour of collecting and combing, my head was fumigated. This involved wrapping my paraffin-ed head in an old towel and sitting me by the range close to the roaring fire Why I didn't go up in smoke I can only put down to the ministrations of my angel, who must have been beside herself with worry. Later my hair was washed and again dried by the fire, in which everything used, except the comb, was incinerated. My angel made sure I never got head lice again.

Across the passage from the kitchen lived my Grandfather's last 'live in' housekeeper and in the will of my grandmother she also had to be given a home for the rest of her days. This seemed odd because many people had worked for my grandfather, especially here in the house in Rhyl. Her name was given to me as Mrs Short", who had a son who had emigrated, so now she was alone. In a couple of unguarded moments mother referred to her as *Miss* Short, which again seemed odd. When I was much older I went home from school to tea with a new found friend. When introduced to her grandmother I was quizzed about where I lived.

"So you would be George's youngest granddaughter?"

I supposed I must be.

"He was a lad. I used to pick up washing from your house when I was a girl. He said he'd give me a sponge cake for my tea if I came into the storeroom to fetch it. I never went but some girls did. They got more than a sponge cake I can tell you"

She laughed

"So you're his granddaughter. I hope you don't take after him or you'd better watch yourself".

This explained Miss Short and grandmother's desire to look after her. She was taken on as a fifteen year old house maid, grandmother was pregnant most of the time. I expect the young, pretty girl, constantly under my grandfather's eye, gave up one day and went for the sponge cake.

But at eight years old I didn't know all this. Miss Short wore the same black clothes for the two years we were there before she died. No one else ever went into her room, which I was told had a stone sink in one corner and a range in the fireplace for cooking. She never hung out washing and her face and hands, the only visible parts of her, became greyer and more visibly lined with grime. She was never seen without her black hat and resembled no one so much as the Wicked Witch of the West from the Wizard of Oz. I used to play Dorothy and have conversations with Tonto about her in the passage, running for my life with

"Oh No, Tonto, she will catch you. Quick, we have to run!"...

...in Dorothy American when I heard her opening the door.

I would hide and watch her scuttle down the path and into the back entry, hoping for a chance to see into her room while she wasn't there. But it was always locked, even when she was there. My father said that she had been my grandfather's housekeeper since she was fifteen and when he died she probably decided never to keep a house again, not even her own, I expect not keeping things became a habit and she eventually didn't keep herself. Anyway, when she died I was sent to take the dog a long walk and not allowed to see anything, particularly not allowed into the room, even when they had taken her away. Everything had to be cleared out by the council, who wouldn't let anyone near it without a special suit.

Somehow my mother managed to run a boarding house, keeping all the guests above the first floor and away from Miss Short. The Great Aunts helped to serve the meals but this was not altogether successful. They were very portly and slightly deaf, so only one at a time could fit into the approach to the service lift. By the time they had walked there and back to the tables they were unsure who the food was for. It was decided that I was a better bet, being small and agile so at nine years old I began waiting on tables, my role in the family business until I finally left home at twenty one.

People came for a week, so presumably had a bath and a hair wash before they came and went home ready for another one. The apartment bells were disconnected but that first year trays of early morning tea and jugs of hot water for washing had to be supplied to three upper floors every morning during the summer holiday season. After the long repression of the war going to the seaside was enough, bath or no bath. After being retired from duties the great aunts generally kept themselves out of sight except that they appeared and disappeared silently as if on wheels and would be suddenly there, at your side, smiling and soft voiced. This was not a problem in the summer when the house was full of people but in the winter with the old house creaking with the wind and so huge and empty the sudden appearance of a dark figure beside you apparently from nowhere was the stuff of nightmares and ghost stories.

Mother was frantically trying to juggle plumbing improvements, wash sheets, cook and learn to run a business while running a home for aging relatives. The front first floor lounge had the piano and it was empty except in wet weather. The ground floor was a hell of relations, cooking, tin baths, making up fires and mother at the end of all of her tethers. Upstairs were guests who only invaded the front room when the weather was wet. My piano playing improved by leaps and bounds and the world that contained me and my angel developed into a fantasy land where the angel could become anyone at all.

I escaped into my music, my father escaped to run his garage. Only my mother couldn't escape. She had worked in bakeries, cycled to work to keep her boys, married for financial security and found none unless she worked again, had a baby at forty, and a shop, and sent two sons to the war.

She was now over fifty and everything she had done before seemed to have been a mere apprenticeship for pulling this house and business into the twentieth century.

For me it was great fun and a perfect education and development in crisis management. I kept people talking while another table was laid, ran up and changed a bed that had been forgotten, stirred porridge, buttered bread and dried pots. There was no washing machine, no dishwasher, and for the first few years, ration books had to be collected and pages removed to account for the food ordered the month before.. This was a book keeper's nightmare and again, another of mother's job.

After the first three years the aunts and Miss Short had died and rationing was over. I got my own bedroom, the dining rooms were expanded and we could take more people. Each summer two girls came over from Ireland from an agency to work. Suddenly everything became easier. Mother began to make lots of money because holidays were accepted as necessary for health and happiness and bookings flowed in. Spain was still only a place in the geography books and the English holiday resort boomed.

Out of the holiday season my parents were loving and attentive, but still busy. So while they were both at home all the time the house was open for me to come and go, knowing there was always at least one of them about. There was always something to do. In the house I could help my mother to decorate bedrooms, an ongoing winter occupation. She still baked for the family and for friends so there was weighing and licking out bowls and blanching almonds and beating royal icing with white of egg and lemon juice. I was not allowed to do the mixing as I never developed the 'feel' for cake mixture.

When mother became fractious and I had played the piano enough I could escape to the garage behind the house where my father would be working. The main space provided garaging for some forty cars. Few people had cars and even fewer used them to get to work. Even the most expensive cars were rust boxes and had to be in the garage as much as possible. When it rained mother ran for the washing on the line and father ran to put the car in the garage where it was leathered down before being left dry. Cars that came on holiday had to be put away in the evening after a family outing. Local residents would have their cars garaged during the week and take them out on Saturdays and Sundays. Even with precise records of this movement of cars and someone to monitor it there was great scope for having too many for the available space. Dad was loving and funny and generous to a fault but thoroughly disorganized. Having lost a couple of sets of car keys and given clients the wrong ones he thereafter asked for cars to be parked unlocked. When he overbooked, which he did almost every week, he and I would push cars back and forth to gain that extra few inches to make room for them all.

Besides the main space there were three other smaller workshops and a loft, all full of Victorian rejects thrown out of the house by my mother

The garage

in the name of progress and squirreled away by my father who had grown up with all this stuff. I moved the mechanical paraphernalia of bikes and motorbike bits, old car tyres, jacks and bumpers and arranged the furniture and ornaments amongst the grime, old oil and cobwebs, Curtains and lace chair covers became cloaks and skirts and I had yet another fantasy world.

The holiday season lasted four months and during that time there was no peace or privacy. A bigger hotel would have had private quarters for the family but the small holiday houses were about packing them in. The holiday makers lived with us and around us. Quarrels, family feuds, tears and tragedy all had to be hidden from the hordes of people that tramped through our lives. One had to be good, and always clean and cheerful. It taught me to hide my feelings. I started to menstruate during the summer months and hid it until the autumn, knowing I would have to find out somehow how to deal with it because everyone, especially my mother, was busy and stressed and trying to stay on their feet and anyway there was no moment in the day to approach it. Instead I stood outside of the local chemist for ages wondering what to buy, but decided against going in because he knew me and would tell my mother and I didn't want it discussed over my head. In the end I laid a careful plan to 'cover ' the situation. I casually told one of the girls working for us

"I started this morning and haven't got anything. Have you any spares?"

When she stopped what she was doing and asked me if it was the first time I assured her with a smile that it was absolutely not and she fetched me the necessary pad wrapped in a napkin. Having solved the main problem I went on my bike to the Boots in town, knowing I could examine the shelves and work out what I needed without discovery. It was September before my mother knew and beyond the time for discussion. In the years of growing up in the boarding house I learned to hide my pain and manage it myself. This was to prove a two edged sword.

Out of the season all the space of this great house was mine. The small garage was my stage and the big garage my dance floor. I paraded down the curving central staircase of the three upper empty floors in mother's long frocks sweeping into the big front rooms overlooking a stormy sea beating up the seawall and spattering stones on the window panes. Outside; miles of empty sand with wind in my face. The dog became a horse and I galloped him across the desert escaping or chasing after horseman. I had total freedom to roam; provided I came home for my homework, meals and piano practice.

My mother's quest was never forgotten. A piano teacher was found the moment we moved. She had teeth like a rabbit and her lips were never closed. When she spoke to you she put her hand up to her mouth as one did to cough in order to protect you from the shower that accompanied her speech. This was not necessary when she was teaching but the end of the piano where she sat was continually washed and then wiped and was a different colour from the rest of the keys. Like all serious pupils I was entered for yearly examinations and collected certificates to monitor my progress. By the time I was thirteen I had passed all possible grades and my teacher spent the remaining four years of teaching me passing on her love of Beethoven, for which I shall be forever grateful.

Mother decided that I should be 'groomed' for my impending career and to this end I was taken regularly to Liverpool to buy me clothes appropriate for a girl with artistic leanings. My school uniform was obligatory. I had passed my 11+ exams and the local grammar school demanded total school uniform down to socks and knickers and this saved me during the week from the image my mother had of how I should look. But my choices at the weekend had my mother's plan in mind, a plan she could not wait to see in fruition and my clothes were generally too old, too sophisticated and so did not really fit my awkward developing figure. I would stand meekly in C 'n A while mother rummaged through the racks for what she imagined she wanted me to look like. At thirteen I was neither the shape nor size of most of the chosen skirts blouses and dresses. They were fussy, extravagant and after she had made her selection were purchased in twos and threes in different colours. Long dresses were bought for me from about the age of nine as mother and father were members of the Hotel and Boarding House Association, which held 'do-s' all through the winter. I was dragged along in my tight pink taffeta, dancing with my father to 'Old Time and Modern Sequence' Joyce Grenfell style.

My school had no music teacher, no orchestra and no means of playing recorded music except for a large old fashioned radiogram that stood on the school hall stage. Its close lid was now used to hold cups and shields on Speech Day. I never hear it played. However, this was a Welsh School. Every festival, every speech day, every assembly of every kind was accompanied by singing. The weekly compulsory music lesson was taken by a variety of subject teachers who taught music as a second study. In fact there was no specialist music teacher at all, but music thrived from the interest and emphasis on music across the whole school. In Welsh Schools in the 1950's there was a policy that music was one of life's fundamentals and to be accessed through singing -

"We are gathered here today in the sight of God to sing our little hearts out – and you boy, third row from the back. I see you and you are not singing. See me after school!"

In the six years I spent in this school five people went to premier music colleges to study singing and numerous others went to study other instruments.

In a school with no music on the curriculum and no official music teacher? How come?

When the school sang, all the teachers sang. They were all there on the stage facing us and seen to be doing it. None of the school had any doubt that the senior master, who was a lay preacher, Welsh speaking and the one who picked out the senior boys for not singing in assembly would just as likely metre out the same punishment for the staff. So every morning we raised the roof to keep the smile on his face.

The same senior master announced at the beginning every December that there would be practices on such and such a day for *his* choir. *His* choir consisted of the whole of the sixth form and anyone else he wished to recruit. We practiced for a month in our own time and then turned up on Christmas Eve outside the Town Hall to sing around the town tree in full school uniform. To not turn up was unthinkable, but anyway we enjoyed it.

Then there was the Eisteddfod. Each class was sectioned into four houses. Every year there was a house competition – an eisteddfod - in the tradition of the bardic roots of welsh culture. Everyone took part., No Olympic race could ever be as competitive as that inter house sparring. The competitions all related to the use of the voice in its various expressive modes. Each house was required to produce a one act play, a choral speaking, a choir and individual items such as instrumental solo, solo singing, recitation, a speech, singing a quartet in parts, writing a poem.

The play production was the ultimate decider. When the whole school had sat out individual playing, singing and reciting all morning we had dinner time and then trooped back into the hall to see four one act plays, directed, costumed, and acted by members of the four houses. The whole school sat wrapt, each child having personal involvement by lending clothes or props, by having a best friend in the cast, by seeing the marks on the board and knowing that this was the opportunity for your house to win because so many marks were awarded to the play.

Did you volunteer to sing a solo, play an instrument, recite, learn a part, and paint scenery? Not really. It was more a "What are you going to do?" than a "What can you do?" Selection could be pretty arbitrary. When a soloist was needed for the song competition and I was not yet involved, I was it. It was a welsh folk song, 'Y Fwyalchen'. I was in the second year, twelve going on thirteen. I had been in the choir but never sung on my own.

The fluttering was there just as it had been when I was five and played my first grand piano, but I was safe and supported by my angel. We stood together looking at the mass of the school while the two teachers at the back of the hall waited for quiet.

"You may begin".

As I opened my mouth to sing "O gwrando…." something happened to my voice. It seemed to go right inside of me to the very place where all of the fluttering was happening and the fluttering stopped. My voice seemed to be a tangible thing that I could feel like you feel hot or sweaty, but neither of those. I felt so strong, like I could put my arms around all those children in front of me and pick them up as a body. I felt like when we finally got a car moving in my father's garage and yet I was not pushing anything, not using any effort at all. Then this amazing noise came out of me and all the little noises of shuffling feet and sniffing and ticks of boredom stopped and there was no noise but my singing. But *I* was not singing. Someone was singing *me*. My angel was finally showing herself, making herself clear. She was not my music. She was my voice. Everything we had done together had led to this beginning, when she could finally let me into the secret. In the time it took to sing two verses of one Welsh folk song my voice became my instrument, my piano playing forever accompaniment. From now on I would play it because I needed to play the music I sang.

The power and passion I experienced that day was a stamp on the rest of my life. Although only in the third form I saw the faces of the sixth form at the back of the hall, always cynical, always putting down, now stunned and compliant. The teacher's faces looking at me differently, quizzically, thoughtful. I had been a girl in 3B with fair hair. The whole school knew me now and it coloured every relationship I had with everyone for the rest of my school days. Beyond the family no one had ever seemed to notice that I played the piano but I had sung once and made everyone think.

Opportunities to sing came regularly after that. At school I would be part of speech day or the carol concert but this was a small town, the teachers were in local organisations and soon I was singing in local churches and festivals. The range and style of what I sang was governed by what I could learn musically. I assumed I could sing whatever I could play and certainly it seemed that I could. I had total faith that my angel would put a stop to anything beyond my voice so I said 'Yes' to everything and waited for the admonishment that never came. Because the voice just came whenever I wanted to sing I had supreme confidence and nothing ever happened to shake it.

My mother was ecstatic. This was more than could have been hoped for. The dresses, the glamour, maybe even stardom must surely be mine. She worked with renewed vigour, the business boomed and my parents became 'well off'. The next move was to get my voice trained. A singing teacher was found who ran a ladies choir. It involved my having a long blue dress and red cape and singing two and four part harmony at 'events'. In return I received a half hour lesson once a week. This lasted two weeks, fortunately the dress had not been ordered. Two lessons of stiffening myself while I took great gasps of air and sang scales was not my idea of either music or fun. Also the woman had a shape like a turkey, a huge bosom and bottom and stiff little legs. I could see this interrupting my hockey playing – my other love - and my angel said "This is not for you".

The other option was a tall haughty lady with hair swept immaculately into a French pleat, who played for the local dance school and all the May Day festivities. I went along at the end of dance school to sing to her.

"I don't know anything about singing, but you seem to. You do it very well. Who taught you to do that?"

"No one, it just comes. I just sing"

"Well while it keeps doing that we'll just let it alone. You can come and sing with me once a week for five shillings. We might do an exam."

Now and again she produced a syllabus like my piano syllabus and ordered the songs. I learnt what was required and passed each one with distinction, but the real joy was being introduced to all the music she had played in various orchestra pits in variety, music hall and musical plays. Through her I was introduced to the music of Ivor Novello, Noel Coward, Gilbert and Sullivan, Gershwin and Berlin. While the ladies choir stood in their dresses and capes singing arrangements of classics I was entertaining the people in my mother's boarding house playing and singing at supper time, or an item on the bill at the local dance academy winter spectacular. Now mother came into her own. She could dress me up.

School, waiting on tables, playing hockey, riding my bike to and from school were not interrupted by this, neither did they need to be. Singing, whether for mother's guests or for a bigger audience was as natural and easy to me as the rest of my life and I loved all of it. Music exams, school exams, came and went. I felt charmed, lucky to have everything I had and happy as a sand boy.

Fifteen came and went. Sixteen came and with it a danger I had not anticipated and nothing had prepared me for. In my imagination there were heroes who came and conquered and loved me but they were out of the stories the music wove. I was safe in the music stories, the dressing up, the play-acting and when I stood to sing my voice opened up all that was there inside me and made it unconditionally available to my audience. Of course I did not know this at the time, just that audiences faces were soft and smiling when I sang. After performances people would tell me how lucky I was to have a beautiful voice and that I was blessed, and I began to look upon my singing indeed as a gift. I did not know why I should have it, no one in my family sang like I did. Mother and father sang along to recordings and we all danced and sang to numbers like 'Tiptoe through the Tulips' on 78 records my father regularly bought from Woolworths.

But I was attracted to grander melodies that stretched my voice and tickled the whole of my body. I loved the harmonies in the music that changed the colours in the melodies. I was fascinated to hear these changes of colour happen in my voice as if by magic if I played the accompaniment and sang to it. I sought out the music of love unrequited, romantic, and desperate. Any kind of love would do as long as it was musically passionate enough to thrill me.

I was growing up and developing musically in parallel with my fifteen year old body, but although I was musically sophisticated and experienced, behind this musical facade I was personally naïve. I could express emotion and had no fear of doing so before a large adult audience. Amongst my peers, amongst the boys of my age, hungry for sexual conquest this must have been viewed as at least challenging, if not 'easy meat'.

By the time I realised that my angel was not going to protect me from life I was falling in love as easily as singing about it. For me the flow of feeling was a natural river with no ebb. My mother should have made me safe but she was hooked into the dream and saw me only in bright lights, her beautiful talented daughter out of school and in some magical world, admired and cosseted. Her life had been so hard, so dreary. My father's sexual exploits began with my mother at forty and he would no more imagine the animal lust of the sixth form boys than believe his precious daughter would indulge in the gropings on the back row of the pictures. I should have been protected by someone who knew about the effect of music on the person who plays it, but there was no one. Later I saw why people who displayed remarkable early talent needed to be isolated in schools of music, but I also saw that I must stay with life if that is what I wanted to express.

Graduation

We laughed and chased each other down the sands,
We were alive and careless of it;
Wanting no more but to probe and touch whatever offered
Out of books, friends, sea, each other's hands.
I gave you my insides after that ice-cream on the beach
Giggling, embarrassed by the bleeding and the smell,
But wanting you to do it, wanting to be experienced
Not a laughing girl, but knowing more.

After it I did not know at all.
You were not changed, you did not love me
As I thought you must, after that gift.
But did we give at all?

Why was I not told by anyone who loved me?
Not mother, father, teacher, brother, God -
That it was possible to give my soul away
And not for love or for a life together -
But just for ice-cream.

Chapter 3: On my own

My sixteen year old peer group was in constant discussion about careers, universities and what happens now. There was never any doubt what I would do, merely how I would do it. I wanted to sing, had to sing and nothing else would do. I had all the qualifications to go to a music college, by the time I had finished my O'levels. I just needed to be accepted at an audition. However, I could also go into the sixth form for two years and read music at University. Suddenly my mother and father were divided over me, or at least the division finally became clear. My father wanted me to stay at home for two more years, or that is how I saw it. Mother became angry at this apparently negative attitude

"She has extraordinary talent. What is she waiting for? Why do another year at school? She needs to get on with her life, apply for the best places now".

My otherwise compliant father challenged the speed of this progression. He had stopped my progress only once before. A roller rink had opened in the town and I was hooked. I had always roller skated. With miles of flat promenade it was a gift. I had skates that clipped onto strong shoes and belonged to a gang who terrorised the local promenade inspector. 'No cycling, no skating' was the notice at either end of the prom. But this was winter, the prom empty and windswept, no holidaymakers to annoy. Still the crotchety uniformed official on his council bike pursued but never caught us. The rink was roller skating of a different kind. You had white boots with attached skates, special dresses with tiny circular skirts and music to dance to. You had your hair 'permed' like all the other skating girls. There were lessons in figure skating and you had a boy partner. Speed skating, pursued by, but beating the promenade inspector was suddenly crass awkwardness. I began to hang round the open air rink after tea and have to be fetched home. This was the very first time that music and singing had slid into second place.

I wanted the boots and outfit and most of all I wanted to learn to lift my leg behind me and spread my arms and dance in my white boots to the music. My age group became divided across the whole town into those who spent every evening gliding like swans round the rink and those who didn't. There were competitions, displays and visits to other rinks. The rink was in sight of the upper front windows of the house and much later than I was allowed out I could sit and watch miniature tinker bells float gracefully and prettily under the lights until nine, when the rink closed.

I never got the boots with skates attached. Mother would have complied but my father's argument was that I was skimping my homework to go to this rink and what for? I had enough in my life already. He rose with a power I had not seen before and axed the rink. I was so angry, especially as I had decided I needed to cut my hair to be a skater and father was against this too. Short compacted hair stayed in shape while you whirled on one foot.

There was a family compromise. I gave up the skating rink and father let me have my long plaits cut off. I was hooked up to a machine that heated my hair and burned it into subjugation. Without my plaits and with these waves and curls I suddenly looked very grownup. The addition of high heels and a pencil skirt and I lost my school girl image. My voice had always sounded more mature than its years and now I felt I looked the way Isang. Now I could be my musical age, I could be as sophisticated as the music I played, the emotional charge I had developed. Only my father saw the trembling inner core that needed at least two more years at home to gain any stability.

More than ever I wanted to get out and use my voice in new places. I was in a small town and there was an expectation that I would sing well. I wanted to sing to a more discerning audience. I did not doubt my ability; I just wanted it confirmed by those who knew about these things. Saturday morning was still devoted to match hockey. Saturday evening Rhyl youth went to one of the three cinemas with the current attachment. I spent my Saturday afternoons rummaging through the solo song drawers in the local music shop, buying what looked interesting and learning anything and everything.

My singing teacher played in the orchestra pit of the Pavilion Theatre in the summer for the annual circus. They were not allowed to have the circus on a Sunday; even animals had their day off. A concert was held instead so that the building continued to pay for itself and the organizers were always looking for items. My teacher recommended me and I earned my first money singing. I received five pounds to sing three

The white dome of the Pavilion, Rhyl

songs twice in the programme, plus an encore in the second spot if needed. It was a fortune. The visitors were only there for a week, at the most two, so only two dresses were needed, one for each solo spot. This time I had a say in what came off the racks in C & A. There was lots of net and low necklines in exotic colours; definitely not suitable for the school dance.

Mother was delirious with pride, my father more concerned that I should

"Come straight home!"

Fortunately the Pavilion was within walking distance of the house. He always insisted on my going to everything on my bike or on the bus, which meant I always had to change to sing and then change to come home. He would never take me in the car and mother did not drive so in this he had his way. I would sometimes arrive at a church to sing a solo wet through and with frizzed hair from subjecting my perm to the rain, but he was not to be moved. At least now we had a bathroom in the house and I could properly prepare myself for these occasions. There was just one bathroom and the visitors were not told about it. They now had washbasins in their bedrooms, but were still expected to have their bath when they went home. Showers were only for the rich, or for hotels much bigger and grander than ours.

At the end of the summer, when those returning to school were beginning their A levels I spent the whole term writing to music colleges. Mother encouraged me, fuelling my dissatisfaction with school, my frustration at the deeper study now required. My essays missed the point, I didn't read listed books for background, didn't turn up for optional extra sessions. Mother sympathised, allowed me to break uniform rules and took my side when school was not pleased.

My dad's challenge to this was to make me clean my bike, help whitewash the garages; anything that got me into overalls and manual work. He and I had always enjoyed doing mucky jobs together. He had an oily dirty garage and part of the fun of doing things with him was to put on the overalls and step out of my mother's dream. Now I too was hooked into that dream and the garage was no longer fun. It seemed that every time I appeared he needed me to change and help with something really gruesome. I kept out of his way, out of his garage. He in his turn began to keep out of the house, coming in only for meals. He seemed to be always grubby and when boyfriends brought me home and I was trying to be particularly smooth he would emerge form the garage in his oily overalls and grunt on passing, woodbine dangling from the corner of his mouth. When I was accepted to study singing in London, missing the second year of my A levels, he had finally lost the battle to keep me at home and grow me up. My school teachers backed him but my head was no longer in the life I had. School was a struggle because I did not want to be there. Nothing was easier for me than singing. Nothing filled me with such joy or made me work so hard. I had never recovered from that first folk song in the school hall, that feeling of sheer power as my voice pulsed inside me and faces changed as they listened.

There were no halls of residence to the college and a bed-sit was found in Tottenham through friends of friends. The income from my parent's business just exceeded the grant threshold so although I received a bursary from the Education Committee to cover fees, all living expenses had to be found. It was calculated that I could live on £20 a week if my rent were paid, which left me, after my underground pass was purchased with about £18.

At my first lesson my teacher looked at the list of music I had sung and rejected all of it. I had sung a Puccini aria for my audition and he threw up his hands and told me to put it away until I was much older. The rest was the collection of songs I had sung at Sunday Concerts and when I offered to sing him 'Over the Rainbow' he smiled.

"We won't do any of that. We have to learn to sing properly. All this popular music will spoil your voice. Put it away".

I was given an Italian song to learn called 'Caro mio ben'. I learned it in five minutes but it was my only song for a whole term. Meanwhile I 'learned to sing' by putting my hands on my professor's sides and feeling the ribs go in and out, in and out and then stay out while he sang a long 'ah.... to the count of five. As he sang this 'ah' he made a long slow sweeping gesture with one arm, stopping as the sound stopped.

"Now you. I want you to imagine you are singing over a rainbow and f_l_o_a_t. the sound".

As soon as I had arrived in London I rang around to find a hockey team that I could play for and Royal Holloway offered me a place in their team. On Saturdays I was tearing around the field and on Monday morning this man who got out of a taxi, arrived at his studio via the lift, and had a body in the shape of a pigeon, attempted to teach me how to breathe.

This was Professor Arthur Reckless, whose name brought expressions of awe when all the new students revealed their tutors. He was reputed to have only the best sopranos and he had me. This was very strong stuff for a girl from a small town. I would have stood on my head and whistled through my bum if he had told me to do it. My life's work was to please an audience with my singing, beyond which I assumed I knew nothing of how to do it. In spite of the success I had had so far I felt I was at the very bottom of the pile here. Every practice room resounded to the sound of voices and instruments. I walked around the building listening to the most beautiful sounds I had ever heard. I was a sponge, empty and ready to soak up all the advice I could get.

"Please take my humble efforts and turn them if you can, into something better. Just tell me what to do. I'm yours to teach and to mould, hungry, yearning for the security of knowing what I am doing"

Here the development and education of your voice was called 'technique'.

I stood with chest expanded by a deep breath, raised one arm, shaped my mouth into an 'ah' and maintained a long steady sound to the count of five, while maintaining my rib expansion as long as possible. This was repeated on about six different vowels while I watched myself in a mirror to make sure I had the correct mouth shape for each vowel. All the exercises involved shaping and sustaining vowel sounds and my ribs regularly collapsed before I got to five. Alone in a practice room standing before the mirror that showed only your face I would struggle for a time and then sing 'Caro mio ben'. That would also fail. I felt no joy in singing it and certainly no feeling of the power that I had always had in my singing. The angel didn't seem to have come to London. She was not in my lessons, not in my practice. Though I would not have admitted it to anyone I knew that she would be with my dad in the garage, I never did get a picture of her going to C & A on shopping trips with my mother.

The struggles to make the acceptable beautiful vowel sounds twice a week for my teacher were relieved when it was discovered that I could play the piano very well and sight read even better. I began to play for other people to sing and discovered a whole world of music besides both 'Caro mio ben' and the apparently unacceptable repertoire I had grown up with. There was Wolf, Mozart, Schumann and Schubert, Russian Opera and Verdi. It was all irresistible and I went out and bought lots of it. At last my seventeen year old passionate soul, starved by one song and lots of static exercises had some meat to chew on. I played it and sang it, egged on by more senior students that I met through playing for them. Apparently everyone worked the college system. You needed the teacher for the influence within the college and for recommendation when work outside was available. Many of the professors were attached to, or performed for, professional organisations. You did what your teacher said but you actually learned to sing by being around the people who could, watching them at close quarters, talking with everyone, going to concerts, learning repertoire so that when a chance came you were ready. The system was there for the exams, the reports and your qualification at the end of the course. The system did not cater for the high flyers but those who would collect their qualifications and step down. If you had the passion and the voice that bound you to performance you were there to meet the right people and to be heard.

This was a complete revelation and I wondered whether I would have been given this advice or met these street wise singers if I hadn't been such a sought after accompanist. I gave my services free. It was worth it. I also realised that my angel had anticipated this because she had kept me practicing the piano when I was young and before I realised how I could sing. She must have known I would need the language of music for my singing and she kept me learning it through the piano.

As a result of playing for senior students my lessons improved. Before I arrived for my lesson I always sang some music that was a joy for me and where I could express my feelings. Then the lesson always went well. I did not tell Arthur Reckless what I was singing all the week, but at the end of the term he commended me on being able to produce a legato with a full even tone and good resonance.

"You can see my dear how it has improved the whole range of your voice to do this work on fundamental technique. Your voice has developed so much more 'support'. This was a word that would haunt me for years..

While still in my first year and without informing my teacher because I knew he would dismiss the idea, I entered myself for the opera prize, not usually tackled until the third year. I sang an aria in Russian from a Rimsky Korsakov opera and reached the finals. While we waited to sing before the principal and an outside adjudicator the other finalists were beside themselves with nerves, dry throats and the possibility of unreliable memories. I stood outside the door and thought of other important times I had sung.

There was the Welsh National Eisteddfod for instance, where every announcement was in Welsh and with my o-level welsh I could only listen hard for my name to be called and step up. I walked to the centre of the stage to sing only to discover that he was merely reading the list for the whole afternoon.

"Not now dear".

Did I die? Nearly. But I won the competition.

Then there were the Sunday concerts for the summer Circus. The animals were in cages behind the theatre but because they had been on stage all week all doors to the back of the theatre must remain open if we were not all to swoon with the smell of urine. The theatre was regularly sprayed but elephant urine in an enclosed space is mighty powerful. Did I swoon? Not Quite. The elephant resided in an open pen and was likely to trumpet loudly or even fart audibly during the performance. Other students may have more musical experience, but my experience had given me something else. I came third.

I'm sure if I had not come third my position would have been made quite difficult but as it was my teacher could not but be delighted. After calling me 'a naughty girl' he picked up the reflected kudos and throughout my career in the college I never looked back. It taught me the relevance of the Ivor Novello and the Judy Garland songs, so now I sang everything that interested me and fired my inner voice. I sang Arthur Reckless what he wanted to hear and I felt he knew nothing of my real ability; that he would not have known what to do with it. He continued to give me exercises to 'support my voice' and I became very successful at these exercises after I discovered that if I stiffened my legs the breath and the sound lasted as long as he required. With stiff legs I could even sing 'Caro mio ben'.

I had unanswered questions about those stiff legs. Why, for instance did I never run out of breath on stage, however physically taxing the phrases? If I had to stand at the piano I avoided the songs known for their smooth melody and 'controlled breathing' because I just could not sustain the length of the phrases. Instead I sang florid, rhythmic songs that were fast. The difference appeared to be in what I did with my legs. On stage I was moving, sometimes dancing. When my legs were loose, I had no trouble singing anything. By the piano I *had* to brace my legs if the support system of breathing I had learned in my lessons was to work. When it did, it was neither comfortable nor even secure. But overall I was being 90% successful. The other 10% would undoubtedly develop with age and experience. Anyway, I didn't know what questions to ask. The only one that came to mind was

"I am being told how competent I am, so why do I feel I don't know what I am doing?"

In my last year I was given roles in the operas the college produced as show cases for their up and coming singers. These are attended by agents, the press and casting directors for opera companies. The Sadler's Wells Opera Company sent for me after one performance, congratulated me but said my voice needed another year to mature. Then they would be interested in auditioning me. The College gave me a scholarship for the year, which was reported in the welsh press. The BBC offered me a concert in their Saturday night series with the BBC Symphony Orchestra in St David's Hall, Cardiff and I sang a Donizetti aria and a Welsh folk song. After the concert Rae Jenkins asked me to return in the autumn for another series. Everything was working to plan, for mother, for me and according to the wizard.

I went home for the last student summer holiday and returned to the Sunday night smell of elephants and working for mother and dad and their visitors. It would probably be the last summer at home and I began to make plans, clear the school stuff out of my room and make a list of things to organise. Better have a medical and a dental check up. Other students had advised me to find a doctor and a dentist in London and I would need advice on how to do that.

I had rarely seen my doctor. Once, at about eight years old I had had worms, excruciating agony of pricking and itching round the bum, especially at night. The doctor was sent for and he told me I must wash my hands after going to the toilet and stop biting my nails because I was transferring eggs into my mouth. I was disgusted with myself at the very thought of the process of eating things that came out of my bottom and terrified school would get to know – this was a small town. Doctors had children and relatives. He gave me some pills to kill the worms and promised me that no one would get to know if I would make a pact with him. Fear turned to puzzlement.

"You must always wash your hands when you have been to the toilet but there is something more important for you to do. You must stop biting your nails, that is how the eggs are transferred and there are all kinds of tensions in your muscles that come from biting your nails. You stop and I will make sure that no one knows about the worms"

I hadn't seen him since. Hockey injuries were taken to A&E and not generally referred on.

I filled in a form and then had an interview. He looked it over and put it aside.

"Anything else? Anything not mentioned here?"

"No, nothing"

"I see two things that concern me and that are not on this form. While waiting for me to read this form you were twisting the side of your face and biting your cheek. You actually used your finger to push the cheek between your teeth. This seems to be only on one side. Would I be right about that?"

I was stunned. I had bitten my lip on the right side of my mouth since I was eleven. I know it was then because the Domestic Science teacher at school noticed and put it on my school report. She also mentioned it to my mother at open day and asked if I were a nervous child who felt insecure. We both laughed at the thought and forgot it, at least mother did. By the time I was fifteen I was not content to chew my lip but pushed the side of my cheek between my teeth as the doctor had noticed. It was a very comfortable feeling to do this. It seemed to have the same effect as the angel soothing and stroking my hair.

"The other is that you are still biting your nails. I remember telling you about that. You should try to correct both of these. If you have nothing further to add, that is all".

I almost didn't go to see the dentist. Again he went back a long way and was the father of the School Head Girl during the year that I was frustrated about being there and being a thorough nuisance. I never made prefect, only vice prefect on probation, a title that put me in charge of patrolling the bicycle sheds for anyone smoking. I felt sure she must have complained to her father about this troublesome half member of her team.

He peered into my mouth and proclaimed me free of cavities.

"But you do have an impending problem. One of your wisdom teeth is impacted. This means that it is beginning to grow sideways because it has not enough room. That must come out and the sooner the better. I understand that you are now on the road to some considerable success as a singer. You do not want to get a few years on in your career and then discover that you have pain in all your teeth and your jaw from that tooth. When can I take it out?"

Instead of seeing this as a blow I was immediately grateful. My angel had scored again. I was home for two months. I could have this tooth extracted and be ready for my last training year with no worries about my health or my teeth. At the same time I would stop biting my nails and chewing my cheek.

"As soon as you like".

Arrangements had to be made. I had to go to the hospital for X-rays and wait for a consultant's report. When it came everything was changed. I couldn't have the extraction at the dentist's surgery because the complicated impaction necessitated removal of some bone. I would be given a date for the local hospital and I would be in for a week. A week! The last part of the report explained the need for the long stay.

'I feel that the upper arch is too narrow to accommodate the wisdom teeth and I advise the extraction of the uppers at the same time. This would leave you with only one wisdom tooth and this would seriously compromise the bite. I therefore propose to remove all four wisdoms under general anaesthetic'.

I had an uneasy fluttering in my stomach, much as I had had when I first played in public and that was repeated when I sang to the school for the first time. Then something happened that I called my angel and I never felt the fluttering again. This time it did not go away. I woke at night and worried but when I mentioned my fears I could not describe why I was fearful. It was put down to fear of hospital; I had never been before; fear of the dentist, I had always been what mother described as 'a fainter'; fear of the pain.

"You won't feel a thing, you'll be out of it and when you come round it will all be over".

I accepted that these were my fears but there was something greater that I felt, but could not express. A week later I was admitted, anaesthetised and everyone was absolutely right. When I came round it was all over. I would not sing with real joy or my own true voice for another fifty years.

How beautiful the evening is,
The sunlight on the grass is still and warm;
Yet full of darting insects, swooped by swallows
Who have arrived too early, beckoned by the glow.
April is not out. The apple blossom not yet drifted.
May waits and yet the sun is hot.
The swallows are confused.
Tulips and primroses are in their prime, a few narcissus linger-
While the first rose opens - pink and summer scented.
"Is this spring, or summer?" sings the blackbird,
"Do I mate, or build, or does this warmth tell me
That I have done all that-
And should puff out my chest with pride
And sing of my success?"
There is a rhythm in a life
For blackbird, primrose, tree and 'specially you.

There is an order and a course you ignore at your peril:
A pattern scored by countless generation and regeneration.
If you should find a summer that begins in April - Stop!
Think, wait! till it be June.
For what the blackbird sings in April is not real commitment,
But just a burst of ego, and a pretty tune.

Chapter 4: Lost

It took a month for the swelling and bruising to go down sufficiently for me to chew normally both sides. As the return to college for my scholarship year loomed I tentatively sang. This was new, I had never 'tentatively' sung before, merely done it and listened to myself doing it. I would then think about what I liked or wanted to change. In a lesson the teacher may suggest changes in approach but if either my voice or my brain felt uncomfortable with these changes, after the lesson I ignored the advice. I still relied on the angel in my head and at my shoulder to support these decisions. She had never let me down yet

My jaw still felt uncomfortable so I always began my singing practice by doing a bit of stretching, opening my mouth wide and pulling it in all different directions. I watched this in a mirror and by the time I went back to London my mouth appeared to open as wide as before. However, I always began carefully and slowly in case I was going to hurt myself by forcing my mouth open. What if I damaged myself? At my first lesson I mentioned my extractions and my fears to the teacher.

"It will take a week or two to put itself right and then you'll be much better for it. In the meantime keep dropping your jaw".

He demonstrated by flopping his head around and dropping his mouth open, looking for all the world like Munch's 'The Scream'.

I began to seriously practice 'dropping' my jaw like this.

Things did not get easier. I had always been able to sing very high and very low so I could sing anything I chose but now the voice became narrower and smaller as I sang higher until it disappeared – poof – much lower than most of the music I sang. Now when I sang low the sound was rough and quite hard. I presented my teacher with the problem and asked if the operation could have been the cause.

"Here are the teeth, here is the voice. How can there be a connection? Not enough support, that's the problem".

He went back to the breathing exercises and held me around the middle.

"There, no abdominal support. Feel me in the middle"

There was indeed a difference between his middle and mine. When he breathed in his belly expanded and as he began to sing this area tightened and became rock hard. I breathed in deeply - something I had not ever had to do, tightened my abdominal muscles as far as I understood it, and tried again. I could now sing high again, not with ease, but with efficiency. I didn't think the sound was very good but at least I was singing the notes. I practiced this breathing in and tightening, also discovering that if I locked my knees as I tightened the muscles I could deliver my whole pitch range every time, no tailing off or petering out. I waited for the feeling of relief and for the joy to return. I waited for the comfort of the angel in my head and on my shoulder to assure me that the last three months had been one of life's blips but I remained alone with these problems. Maybe this was a test to discover whether I could really cut it on my own. Well I had got my voice back and I'd finally learned what this 'support' actually was. Now I could begin to solve a couple of other minor irritations.

The first was that when I sang high my jaw trembled. I couldn't feel it but I could see it in the mirror. In classes, lessons and rehearsals I was told to 'let your jaw drop'. I 'dropped' it with every phrase but had not yet found a way to stop the trembling. I began to modify my repertoire for public performance.

The other was the restriction in my nose and throat, both of which seemed to fill with catarrh. I cleared my throat continuously and when this was noticed in an opera class I was sent to the College Consultant Laryngologist. He was consultant to the Opera House so I was filled with gratitude for the opportunity and prepared to do whatever I was told.

"The nares are too narrow, they want clearing out"

I had no idea what he was talking about but discovered exactly where that was when he pushed an instrument up both nostrils and I smelled burning flesh. I fainted. When I came round he was gone, leaving me to the ministrations of his nurse. Two weeks later my ears blocked with wax and the A & E department of the hospital dug it all out, very painfully. At the end of the term I passed my finals in piano playing but failed the aural. This was a listening and recognizing exam. I had taken many such exams and never before dropped a mark. My tutor put it down to stress, which came as a shock. In all of my performances and exams both in music and in school I had never before been described as stressed. Too laid back maybe, or flying by the ass of my pants, but stressed? Never.

I booked a consultation with another prestigious teacher in the college for a second opinion on my difficulties. I was advised to work on my jaw and my tuning as some phrases were not quite 'on the note'. Otherwise ..." musically very impressive and displays great emotional involvement. A good voice, a pleasing personality..."

I tried to explain how my singing had changed but I got nowhere. I came out without one bit of real help.

There seemed to be no one who recognised my struggle, who could see what I was going through to sing. What had been the best part of my life and the place where I excelled was now agony. I was terrified every time I sang in public, but still I was invited to take on all kinds of work because I had a reputation for accuracy and reliability and for having a lovely voice, good to listen to. I gave everything I could to please, even with the trembling jaw and the tense and frightened body and the audience obviously appreciated that I gave my all. But the cost was high. I began to get sore throats and became quite obsessed with keeping quiet before performances 'to rest my voice'.

Sadler's Wells called me for the promised interview at the end of my scholarship year. I was invited to sing on the stage in the theatre. I prepared and practiced and breathed deeply and dropped my jaw and had never felt so nervous. Only the firmly locked back knees prevented my legs from trembling as much as my jaw, which I hoped they would not see from the middle of the stalls. I never knew what they saw. They thanked me and turned me down. I wouldn't have taken me either. The voice was not splendid enough for this level of performance. The clarity and spontaneity was gone.

No one, not the teachers, not friends or fellow students took me seriously when I tried to identify what I was experiencing, what I was feeling. I received one of two pieces of advice from everyone. From fellow students and friends...

"Relax, its stress. You are working too hard, go out and enjoy yourself."

The other was really worrying. It came from teachers who had watched my development throughout my college years.

"Maybe you are aiming too high. Not everyone is cut out to be a performer. You have to look at all the options and be realistic. Many very talented people with lovely voices get to this stage and realise that being a professional singer is just that one step too far".

For Chrissake will no one listen to me? I listen to others sing and think "I can do better" but I can't get *at* the 'better'. I'm stuck, nothing works, not even my thinking. I can't get to the problem because I don't know what it is. I only know that there is no connection between what I want to do and what actually happens. I can't get my head around it because it is a new and terrifying experience. If only someone, anyone, would say

"You're in trouble when you sing. I can see it. It is because...."

But no-one did.

I took stock. I had to. My training was over and there had to be a plan for what came next. Mother was still on a high and planning my launch into fame, blissfully unaware that any idea of singing for my living was shelving itself. When I finally passed my aural tests just by a couple of marks and completed my piano finals at the end of the year she bought me a fur coat in the C & A sales and assured me that I was never meant to be a pianist and that's why I had failed my finals the first time round.

"There's a destiny working here, you see"

You can't fight that kind of faith.

I took my finals in singing, but in teaching singing because I knew I would need that qualification and was not sure that I would pass the performer's diploma. I read the approved text books, learned the jargon and made lists of suitable teaching songs. Then I mindlessly repeated all the stuff about breathing and support and sang the scales and vocal exercises, not because I believed them to be the way to train a voice, but because I knew that would pass me the exam. In my exam a large female pigeon invited me to demonstrate the correct way to breathe by locating the muscles on her. In a brief flash of clarity I saw that although she was not old her body was very old. She was a retired singer teaching in the College now that her performance days were over. I was suddenly cheered by the thought that I did not need to look like that at fifty because I was giving it up.

"To hell with it all"

I sang better on that day than I had for months and passed with distinction. Maybe I was not a candidate for performance. Maybe I did suffer from performance stress.

When I was offered a summer season on the east coast I couldn't resist having one last crack at it. At the interview I was commended for my beautiful voice and offered fifteen pounds a week from the middle of May until the second week in September. I so needed this kind of praise and it would be fun. No exams, no judgemental stuff and lots of gorgeous costumes. It would also put off the evil day. I decided to do it.

Mother was ecstatic and father was pleased that this occupation that did not appear to him to be a 'proper job' was finally earning me a living.

I suppose it must have been about now that the angel gave up on me and disappeared. There were conversations I had with the angel that I could not have with anyone else because I was this strange beast that was drawn to music above everything else. I had to listen to it, play it on the piano and more importantly sing it regularly or I felt starved and bereft. Playing and singing for other people was also part of my need to make the music. It had less to do with being a performer and more to do with sharing something completely magical that was too big for me to keep within. The music hung in the air between us and we all fed from it and were nurtured by it. I would do anything to keep that in my life in any way because that was my life. With the angel gone I had no one to talk to about my personal relationship with music.

A week of rehearsals and costume fittings in London and then a train on a Sunday out of Liverpool Street to Lowestoft, a place I couldn't spell because conversations on the telephone fixing accommodation had called it 'Law'storf'. The train left Ipswich and the known world to cross a series of mudflats. The guard frequently reminded us over the intercom that if we wished to disembark at the next station we must hurry to the only carriage that connected with that station. These platforms were deserted and I was reminded of Spencer Tracy arriving at Black Rock to face his ultimate challenge.

I was blissfully unaware that I was to step off the train in 'Law'storf' and meet mine.

The East Anglian coast near Lowestoft

"Can I carry your bag?"

A young man was waiting at the station barrier.

"No thank you. I am quite capable of carrying it myself"

He straightened himself and came closer to where he could look down on me from a great height. "I'm supposed to meet you. I'm your taxi, but if you have other arrangements....

I was wrong footed from the start. Apologising, I allowed myself to be relieved of luggage and driven to my accommodation. I continued to be wrong footed throughout the week we rehearsed and before the show opened. It was the one week I had evenings free and he was always there to take me out and show me the countryside. He had a car.

All of my boyfriends had been from my world. They were in my school or they were in music. All were students and none were particularly street wise. Having been surrounded by pussycats I suddenly found myself hunted by a tiger. I had always been a tiger myself, but something had gone from me besides the quality of my voice. I had come here to lick my wounds and gain some confidence and fight back. I did not expect a predator and did not even recognise one until it was too late. I was lost and the tiger won.

Within a week he was in my bed and music went out of the window. Maybe I was desperate to find something that took away the agony and humiliation I had experienced over my voice. Maybe I needed to fall from the pedestal I had occupied since about fourteen because I no longer belonged there but no one would recognise it. Maybe I just couldn't bear to face what I had lost so I just threw away myself instead. A suicide without a death.

A daily timetable developed that revolved around his working hours. My performances were squeezed into this. I found myself preparing his evening meal and then dashing off to throw on my opening costume. Sometimes the overture was playing as I hurriedly slapped on the makeup.

I no longer worried or even cared about my voice or what I would do next. The relief was unbelievably sweet. Lust replaced responsibility; the passion for sex replaced the passion for music. After the show we would drive to the beach to swim and make love on the dunes. All the hurt of the last year, the pain of losing what to me was my life was kissed away. His hands and his body told me that I was desirable and he cared nothing for my singing. By the end of the summer I could perform without thinking once about its quality or whether there was any magic to be had for me or the audience. I merely watched the clock until the curtain came down

I told myself I was willing the curtain to come down so that I could escape to swim in the midnight sea and make love in the dunes because I loved him. The musician needs to please, it is succour to the expressive soul. Not giving of your absolute best is total failure. There is no place, no moment in which you can just be acceptable. Did I really love that he was always there waiting for me and pleased with me. That he had gathered me up and eased my pain. Or had he just gobbled me up?

Some people walk along the beach
Teasing out tattered nerves in wind and spray.
The squawk of gull scudding the water frees the mind to soar;
Releases troubled thoughts, which break like waves
And loose their force like eddy on the shore.
The shore gives me no peace for you are there.
Always, you are always there!
The power, the depth, the endless conflict in my head.
The cliffs, the rocks, all thrust and spray are you.
Me small, you huge and threatening like the sea
Battering my shores and driving me inland.

This bank of grass is warm and soft, cushioning my head.
The daisies smile, the spring-green tree hangs o'er
To serve as cover for a song bird
While the hover fly inspects my nose.
I lie here, spreading wide upon the grass,
Drinking in the evening; the warmth, the softest part of day.
My body rests, mind still and happy.
For in this peace and quiet there is only me
Softening with the evening.
I watch time pass and separate the moments from each other
A gentle hum becomes a buzz
I scratch an ear and pain sears through my neck.
A bee? a being? You are here,
There is no place to lose you
Always with me. Here and here and here…

At the end of the season he wanted me to stay. He wanted to marry me.

My parents came to see the last night of the show and take me home. They had no idea until then what had transpired. I could not tell them. He told them, at least he told my mother. She went forty feet in the air and when she came down she sent my father out of the room as if to protect him from the fallout. She then launched into a speech that warned of the coming of Margaret Thatcher in its cold steely destructive force.

I wept and pleaded with one and then the other but there as no doubt in my mind who would win. I went home with my parents and never saw him again. Mother answered all calls and spoke for me. I never managed a word at all. Apparently I didn't deserve one. I had stepped out into life and created a disaster after all I had been given.

"This will probably kill your father!"

In my naivety I could not know that people do not die as easily as that and only much later I saw that it was mother who was devastated, father just wanted me to be happy. In losing my way I had lost her *her* way and the whole purpose of her life. Somehow I had to find a place for myself that would solve all of these issues.

I began to sing locally and found a manageable level of performance. My jaw was still troublesome, but the sound, which had been unacceptably thin for a professional career was sought after by local choral and amateur operatic societies. There was so much hurt that singing anything with others and without judgement was pain relief and mother gradually accepted that this was it. Regional fame was better than nothing at all. I applied for a post teaching music in Liverpool and was taken on as a probationary teacher, four days a week as I had no actual classroom experience. The board of governers would probably not have appointed someone whose last employer was a summer show called 'Dazzle', but it was January, the music teacher had fled and they had no other applicant. I asked Liverpool Education Committee for another school to fill my week and was given St Anthony's Catholic Girls School, Scotland Road. All the other teachers were nuns and again the post was given to me by default, no one else would do it. I borrowed my mother's car to impress at the interview and came out to discover wiper blades, wing mirrors and number plates removed and preschool children of the area sliding down the bonnet and wings with their little hard shoes. I learned my classroom skills by surviving at this school.

The first Friday two girls approached

"Wherez youz live Miss?"

I said I had a bed sit

"Oo duz yuoz shoppin?"

I said it was me.

"Youz give us the money an a list and weez'll do it Miss"

I had always believed that you get the best out of people with trust and fairness and felt trapped. I accepted the offer, realising it was probably the end of my money.

The shopping came back, the best vegetables, prime cuts, all from the market and for half the price. I was touched and ashamed that I had doubted their honesty. They were just better at day to day living than I was. I repeated my astonishment for Sister Audrey.

"They probably did not pay for it. What they said you spent was actually their profit. We have to be careful. Best not lead them into such ways again".

I slunk.

But could these girls sing! Something about the Liverpool accent meant that when you actually opened your mouth and put your words to a tune the voice, which always sounded nasal and slightly Irish in accent, opened up into an expressive outpouring of resonance and joy which I envied, because that is exactly what I had lost. In the evening, taking myself a walk by the river I would meet these jubilant songsters 'darn the pier'ead', saucy and man catching.

"ello Miss, yu oright?"

There was one more move to make before I could be 'oright'.

I was twenty three, all my friends who had been to University were now settling into marriage and mortgages. The ones who had stayed home and gone straight into work already had children. I had stepped out of the life pattern of girls of my generation. Professional musicians practiced, developed and rode out times when work was scarce and life difficult. You moved, travelled and concentrated on the next move after this. If you met someone whose life was similar to yours, or whose work brought you close, relationships or even marriage happened, but there was no life pattern. Now I seemed to be the only single girl I knew. Worse, I was the only single girl my mother knew and all her friends had wedding photos to prove it.

I married someone I had known since I was fifteen who had as much confusion about life as I had. Neither of us had whatever was needed to sort out what we should *really* do next, so we ducked out together. We were from the same school, the same town, the same world. He became a teacher as a safe option and so did I. I continued to sing and the amateur world of music was delighted to have me. We should have been happy. We had both stepped down from worlds we knew would have overwhelmed us and we shared the relief of that. But for me the peace and security would be temporary. The voice problems were not going to go away. They were going to spread from my music and bedevil the rest of my life .

The Singer

The room was dark, low-ceilinged, full, with nowhere to sit down.
The drinks were passed and spilt from bar to crowd as mikes were set.
Why had I come, packed in by strength of numbers with no power to get away?
And then this girl got up and sang. No, not a girl - a woman quite.
She sang of loss, her body joining with the rhythm of the song.
Within the crowded room she opened up the space
We cannot fill with anything at all we can lay hands, or mind, or tool upon
to fashion in our favour.
I leaned against the bar and listened to her song,
And wept for my own loss discovered in that moment.
If I can stay here with the loss, the weeping and the song,
There may be something of myself to find.
If not - O sing again until I do.

Chapter 5: Falling

I was late, something I could not afford to be on Monday morning. My first student appeared at 9 am for a singing lesson in the Arts Centre of the University. Six half hour lessons with different singers brought me to noon. Six more commenced at 12.30pm a mile away in the department of Education. If I kept to a tight schedule I could leave at 3.30. My little girl's afternoon school finished at 3.45. By the time she had gathered what she had made that day and found her coat it would be 3.55. Monday's were very tight.

School dinner was 50p per day and no change was given. Five days worth had to be given to the class teacher on Monday for both children. I had to remember to collect 10x50p's every Saturday. I captained a hockey team and therefore collected match subs that provided 50p coins. However, Saturday afternoon was my time and my brain blotted out Monday's dinner money. I often mindlessly handed in all the 50p coins.

Halfway through plaiting my daughter's hair on Monday morning I remembered the dinner money. I would have to send a note of apology and just one day's money. By the time I had written the note and gone through pockets for two 50ps ten vital minutes had gone by. And the plait had undone itself.

On good days, days with no squeeze on time I allowed my eight year old son to cross a quiet road by the school himself, but agitation was passed down the line and this morning both children clung to my hand. Today I had to park and take them both to the gates, then wait for a way into the traffic. Five more minutes lost. Then I was lucky with clear roads and green lights. I swung into the back service road of the University at 8:57. This saved a tour of the campus through the one-way system. Provided my car was tucked out of sight clear of the loading bays there was no problem and I would be able to exit quickly at noon.

I grabbed my briefcase, three or four books and music scores to be worked on that morning. Music was cumbersome, not carrying size. It was raining gently as I ran along the path around the side of the Arts Complex. A set of twelve concrete steps led down to the back door of the small Theatre Bar. From there a short cut across the theatre foyer led to the small concert hall where I would teach for the morning. I had often made it in three minutes, sometimes in two.

At the top of the steps my heel made no contact. I half staggered, half fell, arms splayed to save myself, snatching for wall or handrail. My feet gathered momentum, occasionally contacting step or edge of step, but never with any certainty or grip. Anyway, my body was moving too fast. Hands and feet finally abandoned me and I landed clumsily at the bottom; left shoulder and the back of my head thudding against the door of the bar. My briefcase and books peppered the steps.

My handbag emptied its untidy contents: old lipstick, a not too clean comb, coins, stamps, letters, keys. Then everything stopped except the rain. Silence, shock and moments later, unbearable embarrassment. Oh God, how awful. Get up! Speak!

"Howstupid ... musthavetripped ... Yes ... I'mperfectlyalright ... fine ... yes ... really no ... Imustgo ... Thankyouno ... Yesthosearemine ... nonot hurt ... really ... so silly ... Thankyousomuch". Escape.

Gather belongings and escape across the Bar away from these staring, embarrassing people and into the small, dark concert room where, thank God, the first student had left a note about an essay which must be in - profuse apologies. There were no windows in the small concert room, only spot lights. Two were focused on the teaching area. I put down my muddled belongings and moved into the light to examine my knees. Tights gone, well that was to be expected. Apart from that not a great deal of other damage. A bit of grazing on one bloody knee - but soon cleaned up. With a bit of luck my long skirt would hide it all until I got home. I combed my hair, washed my hands and settled down to practice some tricky accompaniments.

The rest of the morning was good. In the second lesson there was an exciting moment. A girl struggling to gasp for breath in the florid passages of Handel finally came to a miserable halt on the third page. She looked so uncomfortable standing there, stiff and exhausted with her failed effort so I suggested she sat down. All the chairs were stacked – there being no concert – so she sat cross legged on the floor. As she now looked so much more comfortable I suggested we tried it again down there 'for fun. When she sang in this position she stopped fighting for air and the singing came easily. We both felt we had created sufficient distraction to relieve the problem, whatever it was and we ended the session laughing. She went away feeling good and I felt my bad start to the day was redeemed. By lunchtime there was renewed spring in my step. I avoided the bar on the way out, not wishing to risk recognition and repeated embarrassment. On passing the top of the concrete steps I was surprised to see how far I had fallen, but the rain had stopped and I always loved the drive to the Department of Education though tall beech trees. I forgot the morning.

"Are you alright?"

Terry was the third of the afternoon students down at the College of Education.

"Pardon?"

"Your eye... have you been fighting or what?"

I took a moment to connect and then felt my face. It was definitely puffy.

"I was in a hurry this morning. I slipped in the rain. I'll have a look at it when I've time"

"You're going to have a right shiner".

Down to work and end of conversation. I picked up the children from their two schools.

"I'm hot. Can we have an ice cream?"

"I'd rather have crisps. Can I have crisps? What's wrong with your eye mummy? Julie says I can play at her house if I like. Her mummy's at home today. Can I go?"

"I banged it at work. You can go as long as her mummy will bring you home".

"If she can go to Julie's, can I go to the park? You said I could take my bike. Andrew takes his bike".

I rang to check that they were indeed under the eye of a parent and received assurance. Continuous chatter of little teeth, school clothes off, scruff on, two drinks, four feet down the path and the day paused. The pause, I realised, was going to last for a blissful hour and thirty minutes until friends' mothers brought them home.

"I'll have a bath. I'll wallow and take my time. I'll have a drink and lie and soak and drift. Luxury. I won't answer the phone. I'll lock the door. I'll have bath oil if I can find any".

I undressed, caught sight of the bloody knee and remembered the morning. I moved closer to the mirror, fascinated, believing I was looking at someone else. The face I saw was badly swollen down one side and yes, the eye was discolouring. I took off the rest of my clothes and slowly rotated to view back and bottom. A large red weal ran from hip line to pubic bone, one buttock was black, purple and red in patches. Both knees had bled and the right thigh was bruised - then there was my face.

"Christ I'm hurt. I really hurt myself. It must have hurt. All this damage, bumping and crashing against concrete - down all those steps".

The picture returned.

"Twelve steps. Top to bottom. I hurt myself! I'm hurt!"

My head stopped shouting at me and I looked again. The woman facing me spoke aloud.

"You didn't feel it. You did all this and you didn't even know. You didn't notice, you went on with your day".

Then, as though I had not heard or understood, she repeated-

"You didn't feel this!"

For a moment everything remained silent; neutral. I looked at myself, waiting for someone else to say something, but there was no one. As if inviting the woman in the mirror to speak again I put out my hand and touched the glass. Either the cold glass, or the reaching out to that hurt let something go, released something down deep in my stomach and it sprang, or gushed, or opened and suddenly gave way. Everything that followed was connected to where the spring, gush, opening, giving way began.

My knees received the message and I slid one hand down the wall as my legs buckled. When I was sick I couldn't move to empty into the bath;

only hang on to the towel rail as my stomach twisted and turned and heaved. Then there was no more and I pulled myself away from the mess to crouch in the corner of the bathroom crying softly. Exhausted, shocked, I urinated over my curled up legs and feet.

Much later I noticed the noise of the traffic and looked up to where the bathroom window was open a little. A branch from the outside wall creeper had poked two leaves through the gap and they fluttered against the inside of the pane. One leaf was green and the other had a brown scar where it had been caught sometime in the window. No, there wasn't just one scar it had been trapped again and again. I helped myself up with the rail and wrapped myself in a towel. I picked my way over the mess and my clothes to break the end of the branch and throw both leaves into the bin. I closed the window.

The bathroom smelt terrible. It brought me back to life. Memories of children being ill brought back the housewife and mother, strengthening my stomach. I put on a dressing gown and cleaned the bathroom carpet. Now that I was once more occupied, control returned as if by magic, so with the bathroom straight, I carefully removed the robe and looked again at my injuries. I picked up the whisky, thinking back to the time when I had set down the glass on the side of the bath. What was I thinking about then? The kids, the bath, the drink; I could remember it all. I sipped the whisky, still watching myself.

It was inconceivable that I had fallen far enough and hard enough to do all this and yet not felt the pain. I concentrated on what I remembered of the top of the steps, relived as accurately as possible, moment by moment the fall, but couldn't remember feeling any pain. Perhaps pain had no memory. Yes - when I was a child. My mother with her friends ... while I was playing ... listening to the conversation ... "If the men had the babies there'd be no population ... you know what they say - pain bears no memory ..." But that might be evolution's trick to promote the species, nothing to do with falling down steps. Come on, remember. When did you last feel pain? You must have a reference for this somewhere."

Chilblains! That was it. Every year I almost made it through the winter coddling feet and hands but watching them swelling by the end of January. By February I dreaded sitting at home after work, my body temperature rising with the heat of the house. Then came the tight skin, red lumps of toes and fingers and the throbbing, itching, excruciating pain. I can almost feel it now. My feet tightened in dread and the blood throbbed in my fingers. When there was company I would go upstairs in pretence of checking the children and weep in the bedroom, face against the cool wall. Later, I would torture myself, feet in a hot mustard bath. When was the last time? Three, four years ago? I still had chilblains in the winter, but I put up with it now. I seemed to have trained myself to not feel it. What else was I trained myself not to feel?

I looked at myself in the mirror, trying to recall one cry or stabbing moment of caught breath; one feeling of nausea… All I remembered was the disjointed conversation held with the people who picked me up and the embarrassment. I blushed, but now my bruised face turned hot and sore. O God, how deep was the embarrassment. Strange ... embarrassment greater than pain ... I bathed, dressed, put on earrings and makeup, high heeled shoes and a dress. I looked at myself again in the mirror.

"There's something wrong with you. There's bitterness in you, a sarcasm, sharpness, lack of feeling. They connect somewhere. But where? Then there's the singing that doesn't work. That's part of it too".

I looked at my watch. It was 5.15.

"Time for the children to come home,"I said to the woman in the mirror. "But what then?"

Neither the woman who asked, nor the woman in the mirror seemed to have any idea. I was cold and the bottom of my stomach crawled in a way I had never felt before, as if it were stretching itself, pleased to be given the opportunity.

My head reels with the music flooding in my ears.
The cellos dip and wind the melody round my bones
Filling me to the brim with new sucked sound
Snatched from the flutes or clarinets, then flung,
Or ground between my teeth.
Tossed back and forth
I sway and stumble to the music.

There is a different melody I hear within. It is my song;
And sometimes music which I hear outside myself
Will drown it for a while, then match its rhythm
So I hear them both together;
Never quite in unison
And wrenching me apart.

The song I am, and the song outside of me
Must find some common phrase and rhythm
Where one is interwoven with the other.
The orchestra takes up our close duet
And flings it string to wind and back again.
The main theme and its rhythm set; agreed,
If I can sing just once inside and out
With the same music
Then I may sing with ease,
Perhaps for ever.

Oh No! …
The orchestra disbands, goes home.
The room is silent, I am left
To listen to my inner song alone.

For part of my week I taught at a Sixth Form College for music and this term the timetable included The Alexander Technique, whatever that was. It was also compulsory. Whilst discovering this from the school notice board I was joined by a man with a violin.

"I am the Alexander teacher", he said, much as one would say "I *am* the vicar!" "I think you are the singing teacher. We should swap lessons".

I was taken aback by the suggestion but before I could gather myself he had arranged an appointment for me.

"I asked your students whether they enjoyed their lessons with you and they said they did. On that evidence I would like you to teach me. As you have not encountered the Alexander Technique maybe we should begin by my teaching you. Shall we make it Wednesday, 2.30? I'll look forward to it".

He was gone.

How dare he enquire about my teaching skills from my students? How unprofessional. However he left me little choice. And here I was, having reorganised my day because he told me to. I was beginning to see a pattern in all my dealings with other people. I just could not deal with anything on the fly. It was as though anyone could push me off my own position or turn me to face the other way. I would helplessly agree to do things, go places, take responsibility, while at the same time in my head I disagreed, did not want to go, wanted to explain my position.. None of that was said, except afterwards when all decisions had been made, when I would anguish, wonder why I had got myself into this mess but couldn't actually find the moment when the process began.

The singing was the same. I knew exactly what I wanted to do and when the music began I was somehow thrown off the path of my intention so far that I might even come in late, giving the impression to all around that I didn't know any better. Worse, that I couldn't hear and feel the rhythm and respond to it.

The Alexander teacher laid me on a table and I fought a tremendous desire to go to sleep.

"Most people want to go to sleep on their first lesson. Don't worry if that happens to you. I won't be put off".

"No, I'm Ok, thank you".

"You have sunk into your hips. I wonder why".

"Pardon?" What on earth did he mean?

"You should be taller, but you have collapsed into your pelvis and your legs are not free".

"I am a league hockey player. I play for the first team"

My first reaction to any confrontation was defence.

"Then you are using too much effort and getting too tired. That robs you of the real enjoyment of doing anything. Also if you are a singer you are not singing very well with that collapse. You can see it in your shoes".

"My shoes?"

"When you get home tonight stand all of your shoes up on the table in pairs. Put the left one where the right should be and vice versa. If any of them will stand up on their own I will give you £5. You probably put them away close together and do not know that they hold each other up".

I felt anger bubbling up inside me. How dare this snotty little man criticise me as personally as this? What had my shoes to do with anything? If he thought I was going to return the compliment so that he could drop in some observations about my teaching and my voice…!

"Thank you, I have to go now and pick up my children from school" my tone was icy. "I expect looking after my family has caused a certain amount of collapse. I'm not twenty any more. We are all different, all different shapes. I have always been short-waisted. I would like to have been taller, especially in the middle, but we can't all have what we want".

He was smiling gently and nodding as I spat.

"It wouldn't do for us all to be the same. Pleased to have met you".

All the way home my cheeks burned. I raged to myself and practised aloud our next encounter at the school. My stomach fluttered again, but I decided it was anger. Flat out anger. I was early home and made busy with all kinds of unnecessary things to do until I could resist it no longer. I took out all my shoes and stood them up on the table. They immediately fell over. Only the flattest shoes would stand on their own but the lean inwards on those was horrific. All the anger and the lesson had left me feeling very weak and I cried, not angrily or hysterically now, but helplessly and hopelessly like a forlorn child.

When this Alexander Teacher told me to reorganise my day, I did it. When he instructed me I followed his instructions. When the guy in Low'stoft had come in for the kill I had meekly allowed myself to be eaten.

I couldn't face my mother with my failure, so I hid the failure, changed direction and got married, when I should have stopped there and then and sorted out the failure. Why didn't I? Everyone thought I was so strong, that I was a tiger, but I began to see that this was to hide the jelly within. When my gut let go in the bathroom I found the jelly within. Why don't I just give up this continual struggle and allow myself to fail? I knew I had to find the strength to do this, but where was it to come from?

You sit there in a blue silk dress;
Fingers curled around a glass, hair swinging,
Ankles sliding through the patent strap of shiny shoe:
While knee emerges, nylon sheathed
To beckon thoughts of thigh and crutch and gasp of breath-
But *you* are falling over, held in place by courtesy of your chair …
You smile around the table. The waiter serves the soup.
The spoon you lift to lip just steadies you enough - the knuckles white -
To carry soup to rose-red mouth,
Returning spoon to bowl, exhausted, trying not to fall-
The man across the table lifts an eyebrow. He has taken in
The hair, blue silk, pale hands.
"Excuse me, is it Peggy?" - "Anne", you answer.
If only you could drop this narrow-lipped control, just once
Perhaps if I could catch that moment when you faltered.
To push, so smile or good behaviour could not save you
From the fall, the hurt, the personal disgrace.

What would you do with energy left over
From lifting spoons and meeting smiles and being good?
What could you do if you were balanced on your two small feet -
Head high, eyes bright, mouth loose and full?
Another pulls the string that spills the soup.
Someone else has wiped the face clean of the smile and shine,
Of everything that made you sing and dance.
So you must just learn how to fall
How to just *fall*
Simply fall
You … must ..... just .... fall.
Or you may, smiling, … *die …*

Chapter 6: Just a Little Accommodation

The bathroom incident coincided with the end of the first year that I had worked full time since having the children. I decided I was overdoing it and it was time I started to take better care of myself. In spite of never feeling that my voice was 'right' I was still invited to take part in local concerts and musical events. I could learn accurately and quickly and turn up for a final rehearsal with a guarantee that I would deliver on the night and although my voice was not as free or as beautiful as it could be it was still a stunning instrument in the musical circles I now moved in. I could have enjoyed the attention, the local reputation and the dressing up as a relief from the hard work of having a family and working as well if only I could have accepted that I was doing my best. In one way I was but I was always dissatisfied with the result and even before the collapse in the bathroom I knew that things were getting worse, the struggle getting harder.

I regularly sang the soprano solos in oratorios for choral societies based in my region and this usually pushed me into work overload for Saturday – the rehearsal with choir and orchestra in the afternoon and the performance at night. Two or three days before the performance I would have to try to somehow reduce my normal workload and get some rest but often there would be extra commitments for either me or the children and as the performance came nearer I would begin to feel my throat dry and uncomfortable. School teaching used my voice constantly and part of this was teaching PE so I was out on the large sports field shouting instructions. The more I tried to save my voice the more problems I seemed to have with it and soon the run up to any performance would strip the resonance from my voice and I would be nervous. Rehearsals went fine but the extra arrangements to get children to bed, myself looking immaculate enough to stand a couple of hours of close scrutiny and get there in time could double the energy put into the day before and the day itself. Even thoughts of 'where to park?' at the venue and getting there on time, things I had always coped with easily, seemed to take on ridiculous proportions.

I began to clear my throat every few minutes to try to get rid of the feeling that there was something continually in it. I thought this was audible only to me until I heard a recording of one of my performances and every phrase I sang was preceded by a tiny sound, not enough for a cough, but still a catch in the throat. It became a habit I could not stop. The only thing I could think of to help me was to practice the support system that I had learned in my singing lessons and as my speaking voice also became troublesome I practiced standing on braced legs to teach. Sometimes in a Saturday hockey match, watching a fast ball come towards me, I would suddenly realise that my legs were braced and I couldn't move until I had let them go. I had always been full of chatter and life was fun. Now I began to sink into introspection and gloom because it was uncomfortable to talk and my body felt stiff and solid. I was developing large hips and losing my waist. I was moved off the half line and given a 'back' position that required less speed and agility.

So here I stood in a rose coloured dress loose enough to take a jumper underneath (churches are cold at Easter) ready to sing Haydn's Creation, having timed everything perfectly, driven home from the afternoon rehearsal to put the children to bed, dressed, returned and parked in time.

There is nothing quite like a live performance; the colours and pulsations of the instruments ricocheting off roof and walls; the collision in midair of the energy bursting from the hearts, lungs, throats and guts of those taking part. No one can respond in a recording studio the way you cannot help responding to people sitting out there, no matter how long a musical life you have. For the singer every cry, sob, chuckle, question or fear the voice has ever expressed should be a part of the sound that explores each crevice of the performance arena, slithering around the necks of the listeners, down their collars, up their sleeves and into their lives.

In spite of my lame voice the rest of me was alive, and desperate to share in this experience. Here in this church, standing in front of the chorus, facing conductor, orchestra and congregation every nerve in me had the same message – to make this performance of Haydn's 'Creation' the best ever heard. I stood for my first solo with chorus, everyone keyed, every eye on the first down spring of the conductor's baton. This was silence with magic.

Sometimes it takes a while to get the right mix. You have to warm to it, allow solo voice, chorus and orchestra to find a balance; a blend. Just as you feel the music "fly" interference can kick in. A late or early entry, an imprecise baton can scupper the interplay of rhythm. A hastily gathered orchestra can just not be up to it. No matter – everyone goes for gold and that, at the end of the day, is what matters to the audience, who feel special in the presence of such commitment.

After two or three phrases I cast around for the specific problem tonight that was preventing this magic. The conductor was peering at his score as if he had lost his place. The orchestra suddenly seemed loud, the space out there very black and solid. I shifted my feet to a stronger position, spread my shoulders and gathered all my strength into the effort that would send a high "C" floating into that blackness, softening it. Then my voice would soar with and over the orchestra, gathering the scattered music together, securing it for the rest of the solo.

I delivered everything I could. It was carefully prepared, poised, launched and delivered. It would compensate with its meticulous musicianship for the incompetence of whatever was spoiling the performance. It would sharpen the awareness of every player by restating the rhythm and phrase of the music. I knew I poured out sensitivity and generosity that brought music to life and that was why I always had lots of work. In those moments when the church felt cold and the seats hard I would deliver that soaring voice. Numb bums would be tolerated, the cold forgotten. I could be depended on to make performances memorable and sell tickets next year.

It took only a few moments to realise that I was singing slightly out of tune. I knew instinctively that it was not to do with any immediate pain, or because I suddenly felt ill. I had given of my best enough times when performing conditions were awful and I was tired and fed up. I was singing slightly out of tune doing all the things I had learned to do. I was in one of those nightmares when you are naked in the street and yet cannot remember getting there let alone taking your clothes off. People hadn't yet seen you but you knew sooner or later they would. With every note the gulf between intention and result became wider. I created a stronger and more precise image of the tune, gathered myself into a mental corset, every facet of my will braced with my body. I tightened all my abdominal muscles harder, braced my legs harder but no effort, no technique, no trick made any difference. I tried them all in the space of seconds. The orchestra still played, the conductor conducted and I still sang, but the muscle system I was bracing was unpicking itself from my brain and as it collapsed I sang more out of tune. . I was back in the bathroom and I wanted to scream not sing, but now there were all these people. As I listened I realised that is exactly what I *was* doing on that top 'C' - screaming. Mercifully the moment had come when the chorus interrupted my solo line and finished the number. (Had Haydn seen this coming?). We all sat down. I felt helpless, hopeless, the disaster of the evening – which had only just begun.

After the pain of this revelation, others followed. During the choir numbers, while I rested from the awful present, the same message repeated itself loud and clear. This had been coming on for months. I was suddenly very 'present' and strangely alone in that full church..

"When did I last really enjoy singing? Ten years ago? When I was little? When I was seventeen? Can't remember, I've shut out enjoyment to hang on to what I have, which now is actually nothing. Did I ever really enjoy it? YES! YES1 YES! No question of that. Singing means more to me than anything. Anything? My children. My children mean more to me.

It's something to do with my insides. All this pain is to do with singing and the pain is inside. My children come from my insides. My singing should come from my insides, but that's not how it feels. There's a clue there somewhere, but what is it? Leave it. I have to sing the duets, the part of Eve with Adam. Tonight! In this performance! Somehow!"

The learning process was quick and thorough. That part of me which had made me special, gave me "life confidence" had finally disappeared and I had been avoiding this moment any way I could. In spite of the practice, the struggle, the braced legs and all the other devices I had added my voice had continued to deteriorate and I had refused to hear and accept it. Every time I got up to sing I was hoping this time something wonderful would happen, the hurt disappear and my wonderful voice magically reappear and give me back my confidence. Well it wasn't going to. This was going to be my last public performance and maybe the bathroom incident was my angel trying to save me from this final moment by showing me that the concrete I had built to 'support' my voice was about to publicly collapse.

This performance proved to the last for which I was paid. Word gets round and I was not asked again to do anything as vocally important. So I stopped singing in public. I still sang and practiced at home for myself but less when the family was around. I played the piano instead. At least there I got out of the instrument what I put into it, although even there I put away the difficult stuff, my fingers seeming to have lost the accuracy they had had when I was fourteen. Still I played better than most and this brought music into my home. Life was full and interesting. The children were growing up and required an almost daily taxi service to and from the activities in their own busy lives. I had more than enough to do.

But I couldn't leave the problem alone. Now I wasn't learning new music and maintaining a role as a 'singer' that part of my brain filled with questions I had no way of answering. Try as I might I couldn't stop asking the questions so somehow I would have to find answers but it seemed I had gone in every conceivable direction. However I had never been to the doctor; my general GP to discover whether there was medical problem with my voice or with me. I had such a history of disappointment that it took a long time for me to make an appointment to see him. I decided not to tell him I was having problems with my singing because most people I knew did not sing and maybe he would just think I was a bit strange. The conversation went like this

"I am a teacher and I am having voice problems".

"What kind of problems? Sore throat? Excessive catarrh? Swelling?"

"I lose my voice"

"And when does that happen?"

"It builds up. It's usually OK on a Monday and I'm losing it by Friday. I also sing, or I used to but performances were a nightmare because again it would start off OK and then I wondered if it would last till the end of the evening"

"That sounds like stress"

"I was always very laid back until I began to have problems with my voice".

"Tell me about your life. What is your day generally like?"

"I have two beautiful children and I teach singing for the University and various other organisations. My work is fitted around my children's timetable so I don't have a feeling that I may lose my job because I'm a working parent. (I knew that many of my female friends with children suffered this and saw the reaction in them) It seems that I can correct every voice except my own. I correct in others what I cannot correct in myself, which doesn't seem to make any sense. I'm very unhappy about all this".

"This seems to hit the nail on the head. That's why you lose your voice. Unhappiness is a terrible stressor and you're unhappy. How old are you?"

"Thirty five".

"It is quite common at your time of life to get bouts of depression. I can give you something for the depression but remember, you have two beautiful children and your life would seem very full and satisfying to most women. Not appreciating the good things in life is a sign of depression. I will write you a prescription for a month and see how you go. Then come back and we'll talk about it some more. I'll give you the telephone number to ring should you feel you need extra help".

What about my voice? "

"Rest it. That's what it needs. If the problem becomes more severe in spite of the rest it may be necessary to examine you for nodules, but we'll cross that one when you come back in a month".

I contemplated killing him.

From being a small child and all through my teens, if anything troubled me I sang. Then I felt much better. It was my secret remedy. I did it when I was angry too. I remember my mother wouldn't let me go out once when my friends were going roller skating. I was so angry with her I wanted to kick her. You know how it gets when you're eleven. I sang through everything I knew as loud as I could and it made me feel so good I didn't care any more about going. I hadn't that gift any more. I don't get that feeling *ever* when I sing. Just fear that this will be the last time.

The car was being serviced so I went home on the bus to pick the kids up from school. I am always fascinated by making a story out of snippets of overheard bus conversation. Two women sat in front of me and one said she had a sister… "Who's the receptionist at the hospital" I pricked up my ears because I knew her sister well, at least I knew her underwear well. The sister lived next door to me. The couple were middle aged, stolid and unsmiling but she was singular for her underwear, which appeared on the line the other side of the fence and would have made Anne Summers blush. He, on the other hand wore long sleeved vests and interlock pants, which took a very high wind to even make them flutter…..

The woman on the bus was telling of an evening she and several friends had spent round at her sisters doubled up with laughter at the noises coming from next door where…

"..this woman was trying to sing. Well you'd think, wouldn't you, that if you made a noise like you were being strangled you wouldn't do it. But she kept on and on. Talk about cats. We were going to bang on the wall but actually it made our night".

That was it for me singing in my own home. The next time I went to practice, which the family ignored as long as I closed the door, I stood in the music room and just *couldn't.* The children had always made faces about my singing but they also made faces about my homemade bread.

"Why can't we have proper sandwiches to take on school trips with proper white sliced bread like everyone else has".

The filling was no good either; it wasn't cheese slices.

So I could ignore the attitude in my own house but suddenly there were others and these 'others' may be there or may be not. I would never know who was listening when I sang, never know who was giggling at my attempts to find this lost voice; mocking my pain. The future suddenly became unbearable. Unless I found a way to solve this problem I might as well get off this bus at the railway station and throw myself in front of a train because I was an empty shell walking about the world with no purpose or meaning to my life.

Woh Silver! You are going to pick up your children from their day and give them their tea. You love these two people and they trust and rely on you. What is all this about opting out? But I knew that if I could not sing I was just a shell. With them my life was full of doing and going and being and growing and laughter and fighting and making up. But I couldn't give them the responsibility of making my life worthwhile. I also had to find something to give that I knew it was valuable. I knew it was there, somewhere. I just couldn't get at it. What kind of courage was I going to show them if I couldn't sort out the only problem I could remember having.

Opting out now would desert them and I could not bear that. Living with this problem, which seemed so trivial to everyone I discussed it with, was also unbearable. I went suddenly cold because I knew I was very close to completely giving up what I saw as a life struggle that I was struggling with totally on my own.

Before I got off the bus I had decided I had nothing to lose any more I couldn't ruin a voice already ruined so I would have one last radical crack at it. I had a friend who was organist and choirmaster in a large local church.

"I need somewhere to practice where I can guarantee I will not be heard".

Practice is the wrong word. Start as you mean to go on!

"I need a place to make noises that no one will want to hear. Terrible out of tune singing which is not singing, except to me. I'm grasping at straws. You must have a key to this huge church. Can I go there and try to discover what is wrong with me. After all - that is what the church is supposed to be about".

He said he would leave the key under the corner of the first grave stone by the gate. There were conditions-

Do not use the church before closing time for the public (9pm)

Do not put on any lights.

Enter by the vestry using the choirmaster's duplicate key

Do not tell anyone what you are doing.

Agreed!

Chapter 7: Hunting for the Cause

I left the house on my bike at 8.30pm. The churchyard was dark by the time I arrived and I wheeled my bike up the path that led through the gravestones and up to the small heavy studded door towards the back of the church. This led into the vestry. It took several attempts to turn the key in a door which had been there since 1100. This was not good as I was looking for any excuse to flee. It opened just in time. I made my way through the vestry, feeling the walls and searching for the heavy velvet which separated this space from the church itself. Once in the church the moon shone through the windows, illuminating the floor. As I groped I talked aloud to myself - a substitute for "Lions and tigers an bears Ha Ha, Lions and tigers and Bears Ha Ha…

"I have to do this. I can't bear anyone to hear the noises I make. Don't be afraid of the dark or the church. There can't be anything frightening here. It's a church for God's sake!" (I had to smile)

But the church was huge, the walls black and terrifying. Outside the summer night sky was lighter and gradually I saw the statuary, the great windows, the pews and the glimmer of the dull red safety lights locating the great cross of chancel and nave. This was the space where I could make my noises; where no one would hear except the sleepers in the great tombs lining the walls. Then the agony would be bearable.

And what of God? Would God mind? Church music was always so divine, so perfect. Treble voices pure and unrelenting. Sex-less tenors, vibrato-less altos, paternal and solid basses. God the Father – rich and deep. Women did not raise a voice in this high church unless to sing of virginity, duty or devotion. I stood in the darkness, suddenly feeling small and tired, unable to beat the programme. I had stood on those steps over there eighteen months before and filled this space with glorious….

NOOOOOOOH!

The word screamed itself out of me and into every corner, every niche and carving. After that I could not bear to return to silence. I sang loudly, incoherently, every thing I could think of. When I couldn't remember the words I made them up, not pausing between the Mozart and the Gershwin in case the echoes died away and left me there alone. All of it was terrible, the throat rasping, the breathing laboured, pitch dropping throughout whatever I sang. I felt like an old elephant trumpeting its last and sinking into the mud to die. My stomach shook and I was back in the bathroom, urinating as I sang, but singing anyway. The tears poured down but I couldn't stop singing, emptying myself of how ever many years when I had been afraid of this happening in public. Holding it back, pretending everything was wonderful. Along side the pain of a strangled throat and a tense body was the sweet relief of emptying that flood of obscene noises, getting rid of them.

Although I felt I was singing it was not singing as I had been taught to understand it. It was more like vomiting. The churning gut; the racing pulse; the distended throat; the desire to grab between my legs and prevent pain, I had wanted to do that in the birth of my son when I felt equally ignorant and terrified of the process. All contributed to the feeling that I was being turned inside out until exhausted I finally sank to the cold floor, laid my face against its stone and was quiet.

Much later, having struggled to my feet and found my way out I locked the door to the vestry determined it should be the last time I put myself through such emotional pain. Was I becoming kinky or what? I rode home to find some other way. I couldn't subject myself to that again. The next day my body felt looser and my voice did not have such a hard edge. I was on my way.

I went back twice a week, after 9pm, all that summer.

On the next visit I tried to introduce some measure of control. I began with familiar scales and exercises which would coax a uniform sound throughout my known vocal range, attempting to ease descending scale passages over those parts of my voice that did not behave as expected. I had been taught to encourage "head voice" to merge with and influence "middle and chest voice". I discovered that none of this jargon made any sense in my particular pit. Even *thinking* about applying it would produce a feeling of pent-up anger which exploded my voice into raucous, uncontrollable noises, nearer madness than singing.

After a particularly tiring day and in a gesture of sheer frustration I sank to my knees.

AAAAAAAHHHHHHHH!

The sound that began as a complaint suddenly felt easy and soared around the church. Without stopping the sound I rolled over on my back and pulled my knees up to my chest. It was as though someone had plugged in a PA system. The 'AH' that I held in my body amplified itself and flooded the church with effortless sound. I stretched myself out and rolled on the stone flagged floor between the pews, singing once again everything I could think of, mixing up songs and arias with nonsense and poems; whoops and shouts. Oh how wonderful. What relief. I can *sing* rolling around the floor. I can feel my buttocks opening up like two full blown roses. I don't know how that affects my singing, but I'll worry about that later. This is the nearest I've got so far to my voice feeling like my *own* voice.

I wanted to move it on, find out how to do it and plug the information into my brain. What sounds could I sing? Never mind words or music. Just let the voice play with – what?. Vowels sprang to mind, but vowels needed colour if they are to be interesting. What colour are vowels? And which vowels are which colours? I saw the colours as my voice swooped and bucked and drifted, squealing miniature high sounds that popped my ears and then descending, touching base on this and that sound that I did not plan, like a gymnast hitting the bar between somersaults.

I painted the church bright blue with "OH" and green with "ER". As I rolled about my voice and body became increasingly loose and I discovered new ways that both could move and play together. I hung over a pew, head down and "AH"ed my way into reds and purples bursting like fireworks in my head. With these vowels I repainted the military banners hanging in the church. I discovered that I could sing upside down. I lay across the altar steps, head hung back as an early martyr, "Eeing" and "OOOing" my dissent; ER-ing my burning body.

A large carved screen hid the choir stalls and the high altar. Its intricate tracery offered handholds and I nervously tested it for weight bearing. The wood was old and black, pickled to the strength of metal and I climbed up it until my whole body was off the floor and upright. Here again I could sing. I slid my feet from their footholds and hung from my arms, clinging in the dark almost in the same position as the figure before me over the high altar. I sang to him, as we both hung, the Alleluia from Mozart's "Exultate Jubilate", feeling it resound down through my whole body and exit through the soles of my feet to flood into the huge blackness of the church behind me. This was it- I had found my voice again. Everything was back to joyous singing.

I climbed down and stood where I had stood eighteen months before with a full orchestra and chorus. I began the aria from the "Matthew Passion" – Break in Grief. It was as if the past half hour had been a dream. The voice was returned to all its harsh ugliness. For the second time that night I fell to my knees and filled the church with sound. With uncontrollable sobbing and howling as if some banshee had taken me over. The crying and howling touched parts of me that the singing had touched, but instead of the excitement and elation that had brought I began to feel angry and bitter. I shouted things to the empty church, cruel, hateful things, rocking myself, arms and hands massaging the anger in my gut. Most of the abuse I shouted at God. After all, I was in his house.

I arrived home at 11 pm. The house was silent and dark and I sat, knowing I must think about what I had discovered so far but not even being able to start to know what that was. The only sure thing was that the problem was not in my voice. My voice was there where it had always been; not ruined; not failed, not having to be found again. It was where it had always been, in my body. But why had I been able to sing when I hung, when I rolled, yet not when I stood?

When I thought about my body and the uncontrollable anger that I had felt earlier fear crawled in my belly. There was an unknown I did not feel safe with, another woman I did not seem to know. Perhaps it was the real me and I was about to meet her. This was the third time in one summer I had lost control. I must begin to know and understand what is coming out of me. I must write these feelings down before another "pain has no memory" became one more life process I did not understand.

I decided to express the sounds coming out of me and stop trying to find out what was wrong with my voice. Focusing on my voice may be wrong. I must find out what is wrong with my body and maybe my mind. But I could only begin with the information I had and that was the sounds I had made. They were coming out of my body and they were terrifying me. Voice, body and mind were together in the noises which came out of me when I hung in the church. I wrote them down in the only way I found possible.

AH.
Vowels are the sounding board for our emotions
And our lies,
None more so than - AH! - the exclamation and surprise,
The scream, the agony, and centre of our woe.
AH! Opens up ecstacy, discovery, panic.
Draws out relief, release, the in-and-out of life supporting breath.
Prevents approach, shuns and shuts out.
You choose the message with the vowel.
The ma-ma-ma and da-da-da of first communication.
We begin – with – AH!
So many of our most important words
depend upon this vowel that opens up the soul -
Gives glimpse of our insides;
like hAHt, fAHt, Ahtery, Ahmpit, Ahse.
And also Ahtificial, dAHling. And is the most important cAH?

OH! …
… resembles AH!
but narrowed into shocked respectability.
What "AH!" would go for straight away "OH!" questions in sedate surprise:
"OH really?" or "OH no" or even "OH I couldn't"
AH spreads the face wide, smiles, exposes teeth, inside of mouth
And opening of the gut -
That vestibule of warm salivary redness.
OH shuts this down, disallowing view of insides.
Says "Hide your teeth", "Make a neat round hole"
So every body knows just where they are -

control, goal, role, soul, camisole,
And 'No', designed to keep us in our place.

A! As in "mat"...

Ma...is the finnish word for ME
ME is soft and self effacing, sorry that I mentioned...
Sleep, weak, Easter, deep, bereavement, easy; all are "eeees"
I cannot think of one good swear word; one gobsmacked rousing
curse
that uses "EEEEE".
So when I talk of "me", "EEE" puts me down;
Removes the strong inflection I would have you see as me
and trails off meekly at the end.
"Please remember me", - intolerable whining.
Will you love me forever?" - puts stress on "love" and "ever", but not
ME
And I am killed by language, stabbed by a vowel,
Undermined by rhythm and the bleating of my voice!

But when I'm MA I stride about and beat my chest
With every glorious phonation.
The vowel strikes my centre back and spreads as hot sun
Through my rib cage; fingering and tickling my heart
To set it all aglow.
MA! MA! MA! I am important, tall with head held high.
In any sentence MA has clout,
"Don't do that to MA!", "Remember MA",
"Will you love MA forever?" You could not be mistaken or mishear,
And later, open mouthed protest your ignorance,
Your arms around another.
"I did not know to whom you were referring ..."

Next year I go to Finland.
The Finns may offer more to change MA with!

"I" as in shit!
Idiot! I told you how we always did it this way.
You used your intuition, which you call "Gut feeling!"
How inexperienced, how naive, how wet behind the ears.
I laugh at you " HI! HI! HI! HI! HI! HI!"
(To do this and experience the thrill:-
Place one hand on your pubic bone - the hairy bit,
The other hand across your tits, or where they'd be.
Don't take in any air, just push the HI! right out with muscle.
A dirty laugh, but so much more -
The feeling that your voice sounds in that place
Where you made love when it was good; the best.
(A secret sticky toffee feeling you will share
With someone sensitive to enter in,
But yet not interfere)

"OO" as in Prude

"OO" is a neat round hole - at either end.
Tight lipped or tight arsed, both say OO.
Vowel form for kissing maiden aunts at Christmas.
Choir boys live their lives on OO and manage somehow
To funnel all their words through this one shape.
And when they reach pubesence, this one shape
Will trap their balls and turn them into
Semi-tenors - clipped for life by oratorio and early music, their pert
round lips -
Obicularis oris - prevents expression that is sensual.
The voices all will be for God, virginity and purity,

Sucking pencils in exams and smoking.
All are silent "OO"s. Dummies, nipple fixation -
OO is what we're after "OO, it's lovely, I can't get enough"
"Whistle and I'LL come to you, my lad"
Now I can see the pursing of your lips in my mind's eye,
And here are mine all gathered up for you.
OOOOO there's Wwwwwwwwonderful!
We hardly need to touch.

"Er" as in erred

"We have erred and stayed from your ways like lost sheep"
("My God! You haven't done that thing again - that thing you
promised not to do?")
"ERRR No ... at least not since the sin was register-er-er-ed.
I do not wish to hurt you or disturb
That cobweb thread that binds us to each other.
I gave my word, and since then, please believe I have not done it.
I listened to your argument. I heard
That you had had enough of me
If I could not concur
With your demands. Your cruel slur
Serves to deter
Me from that thing you dread. I gave her
Up, deter-
Mined to remain forever
True to you!

O Come on, do be reasonable, it's over
This wittering on and on is quite absurd
So pour the G&Ts and Bon Viveur!"

OW! As in pain

Out! I rang you earlier tonight, but you
Had switched the phone off in your head.
I listened to it ringing, but you did not answer,
Did not want to hear my voice.
OWCH! That hurt. Playing games with me as "it"

In my frustration I cried out to empty air,
Spontaneous expression of my pain.
My mouth stretched at the back, my head felt airy, spacious.
I "ow"ed again and mouth distended to my throat - my gut,
I threw more "ow"s at you, my stomach bounced
And my soft belly made itself available
To no one in particular - .
Just available.
Ears beating with the rhythm of my blood
I " OW! OW! OW"ed out all my pain
Until the pain changed to excitement - free-fall from a plane.
Ski -ing off piste has punched these holes before,
But never you.

Don't die for love.
Shout OW! and shout it loud!
You do not have to find the snow
or launch yourself off Beachy Head.
A short sharp shout can also pull the trick.

By now I realised that I was only singing vowels. I instinctively knew I had hit on something important and questions sprang into my head.

"What do you know about consonants? What have you been taught? Go back to the singing lessons. No that's not where you first learned about consonants. Where did they first *become* consonants? The Alphabet! Learning the alphabet. Go back to school!"

I sat myself in Middleton Schools, Harrow Road Infants School in my pink frock with a neat ribbon and a bow on top of my head. My cardigan was grey and pink stripes, knitted by my mother. The grey could be obtained quite easily by saving some from knitting socks for the war effort. The pink was recycled from baby knitting to relieve the drabness for a little girl. The school was one storey red brick and the classrooms all opened onto a central quadrangular lawn. I went at five, walked to and back by my mother and spent all day in this one classroom with the cards on the wall. Twenty six of them, each with a big coloured letter and a picture.

How did you learn your alphabet?

Like this? Ay Bee Cee Dee Ee eF etc

or like this? A Buh Cuh Duh E Fuh etc.

We said the separate letters every morning and then put up our hands to spell a word that began with.....

Next the cards were shown randomly to recognise vowels and consonants:

B: "Bee – Consonant!"

P: "Pee – Consonant!"

E: "Ee – Vowel!"

S: "eS – Consonant!"

No, that is not correct. You can only say 'Pee' by putting a vowel after it. 'Es' has a vowel before it. You have to use a vowel to say a consonant I looked with horror at this belief system I had followed all my life, through my singing, through my whole personal language development. I had believed that you can say consonants, that the *voice* does them. But the voice only does vowels. Consonants resemble a snap of the fingers, a clap of the hands, or a rap of the knuckles against a door.

"What about mmmmms and nnnns, not to mention llllls. Listen! I can make them last as long as my breath"

I walked around the room, listening to these sounds, watching how I made them. A vowel squashed into a space and then trapped there by tongue or lips. When I moved tongue or lips away the voice sprang gratefully into "AAHH". The voice is *all* vowel. There is no personal information in consonants any more than there is nothing in the clicking of your fingers or the clapping of your hands. Both say "Attention Please" but only the vowels can vary pitch, define sex, or express emotion, stability, instability, age, experience, position.....The connection between me and my voice could only be made through the vowels.

Back to school again! When I came to a word like 'B-E-D' I spelled out 'BUH-E-DUH' because I learned to say the letters that way. At about eight I was reading 'Ifu you shouldu meetu a crocadilu' and receiving commendations from teachers for emphasising the ends of my words. Move on – what about the singing? Think. What happened there?

When I was eight my parents moved to Wales, I went to a Welsh School, learnt Welsh and began singing at the age of twelve by singing in the local eisteddfod, in Welsh. These Welsh songs were my voice and language training, I never had lessons except for guidance in interpretation from school teachers passionately devoted to anything vocal. These teachers variously taught maths, science, geography and languages – none of them were music teachers but most were Welsh. I thought of the welsh language and its singing tradition. It was true, there were many welsh singers in the college. Wales had its own college, its own opera company and all those choirs and Eisteddfods. Why was that? A musical nation, that is what people said. But if it was a musical nation where were the conductors, the violinists, brass players? The other major Welsh export was teachers. There were more Welsh than English in the media as well. So it wasn't to do with music, but language. I sang a couple of welsh folk songs and realised that I landed heavily on the vowel for every sound I sang. Every syllable ended with a vowel. When I sang an English song it became too easy to land on a consonant. I remembered struggles to sing the songs I was given in my first year at college and make the words clear.

"Should(u) he upraid(u), I'll own that he prevail(u) And(u) sing as sweetly as the nightingale(u)".

The teacher was only satisfied when he heard every 'd' on the end of every and. I hated every lesson of breathing exercises, diction exercises and rolled RRRRRs – hated the feel of exploding the consonants to project the vowels. I must have gone back naturally to my welsh training of singing from vowel to vowel to sing those songs I did not dare take to my lessons; Passionate Rachmaninov; dark and dangerous Tchaikovsky; Wolf, Mozart. Still more wickedly Cole Porter, Gershwin and the Songs from American Musicals. How strange that these should have been unacceptable.

I took out the copies of two songs from different sides of the musical track. Awareness is everything. I didn't even have to open the Schubert song. I observed the tension build in my body and my throat as I *thought* of singing it. The consonants gathered together as an army to marshal, control and finally catapult the vowels out into the world. I might not even have existed from the neck down. My head sang, my body looked on. I turned with relief to "Fish gotta swim, birds gotta fly..." and the first syllable released my voice to fall and be cradled comfortably and securely by the 32 feet of gut swilling around in my pelvis. Oh the softness and sweetness of singing from there.

I had to learn to sing all the music like this. But How?

When I sang Welsh at 12 I knew that was OK. I had no problems. I just sang. Italian worked pretty well but not as well as Welsh. But I couldn't sing everything in Welsh. I decided to apply the rules of Welsh and Italian to English and see what happened. I wrote out Away in a Manger in the syllables you sang

A – WAY – IN – A – MAN – GER. My mouth closed on 'way', 'in' and 'man'.

I wrote it out moving the last consonant onto the next syllable

A – WAY– I – NA – MA – NGER It worked.

My mouth remained open to sing all the vowels and all the vowels buzzed in my body, but visually it was not very satisfactory because you tended to close your mouth at the end of 'WAY' and you might sing the wrong vowel at 'MA'. Try again.

A – WEH – I – NA – MEH – NJAH Got it!

All the vowels now plummeted backwards and downwards into my body. All my singing training so far had encouraged me to project my words by firing the consonants at the audience and hanging the vowels on this energy. I began to reverse this. As I rolled on the floor or hung from the screen in the church I sang syllables which had the vowel at the end as in welsh. I then pretended I was in Russia and imagined brooding sweeping melodies from the harsh life of the Steppes. I now understood that all languages had to be sung like this. I would use this invented language to sing the classical repertoire I had been taught to sing by exploding consonants and see what happened.

On church nights I couldn't wait for 8.30pm to leap on my bike and experiment with different styles of music, different languages. The differences between the songs stopped being the way I sang the words but how my imagination coloured and highlighted the vowels to give them meaning, nationality and style. Instead of trying to get my voice up and out of the deep pit it had fallen into, taking me with it, I drove my voice down there while I stretched my body and found the place no longer frightening. There was no more sobbing and collapsing. I still could not sing on my feet but there was no panic about that either. I had discovered the window in a hitherto solid wall. It was tight shut, but it was there and what's more there was light filtering through into the darkness I had known for so long.

I was different after that summer. It had changed my breathing, my heartbeat, and how I saw myself. That is what a good song does, so I knew this was the right direction. I suddenly felt strong enough to try sort out the rest of my life.

Moving through our separate space together.
Surrounded by the glass we've manufactured
From the sand of positive indifference,
We pass the time.
Grain by grain we grind it in our teeth,
Then heat and blow it out into a bubble
That surrounds each one and keeps us safe.
Then through these two glass walls
We watch each other,
Sometimes making faces,

Pressing nose and fingers on the glass
And mouthing soundless signals of loathing and desire.
Knowing that nothing will ever break the glass
And shatter our separate security.
For after all the wall was built with love.
There is no strength like love
To build a fortress with.

Within two years I had left home with my children, believing that I had recognised and *begun* to right some fundamental mistakes. I felt confident and sure that I could bring up my children myself. I had a good income from my teaching and had never felt so strong. My thirties were nearly over but by now I had learned some important facts about myself and my voice.

I used too much energy to do everything and this allowed me to avoid important things:

- I was never happier than when I was driving myself like a train.
- I was hiding emotional instability and inability to cope.
- I could not sing standing up but I could sing rolling on the floor.

There was a parallel between my life and my voice and I had to find it.

Chapter 8: Dealing with the Symptoms

I knew I would not be able to deal with the divorce. During even minor confrontations, like the time the headmaster of my son's school sent for me for a 'discussion' adrenalin began to flow even at the thought of what I would say. He and friends had been seen climbing a farmer's haystack and when everyone ran he stayed and gave his name. I was proud of that, said he had done the right thing, which was in my head to say at the interview. But the Headmaster sidetracked me, asking whether my son was possibly unsupervised after school because I was a working mother. I couldn't turn it round and establish a position in which I was not lamely defending myself and subsequently, my son. Yet I knew I was the more articulate, the more honourable. He was not interested in the ability of my son to do the right thing. He was enjoying fluffing his feathers and I failed to control that in any way.

So it was with any discussion that followed the announcement that I wished to end an eighteen year old marriage. I began to describe how I felt, then emotion overcame reason and the words I wanted to say did not come out. Frustration at not being able to express myself ended in floods of ears, hysteria and slamming doors. I would carefully plan what I would say next time, determined to stick to my story and be reasonable.

It was no use. No amount of planning could prevent what happened in my brain, my body and my voice. First my breathing became erratic, as though I had not enough breath to complete even a short sentence, then I became hot, the blood pumping in my throat and speeding up whatever I said so the words tumbled out faster than my brain could understand or process what I was saying.

I could not bear to stay, and I could not discuss why. This was no one's fault but mine and I could only agree that it appeared I was unable to see sense. Everyone around me advised rest and diagnosed stress, even counselling. (Where had I heard that before?).Finally I decided not to discuss it at all in case, as with the Headmaster, I lost all hope of making the changes I knew had to be made. I made clear plans to leave with the children and applied myself to the huge physical task of dividing the household. I began to feel stable again – was it because I had some hard physical work to do?.

I would need a place for myself. It would need to be in the same vicinity so that the children could go to the same schools and see their father regularly. I would need money for a deposit and until the family house was sold, which at the moment my husband refused to do, I had no means to do this. My mother, long retired from the business, had money invested and the obvious course was to ask her to invest some of it in me for the same return, but there was such a history of pressure from my mother. I must make my own decisions and I must not put myself in the path of people who could so easily disempower me. Mother was still in North Wales and her sister, who had also retired from the butcher's business, lived nearby. I decided to ask my aunt and took the children to Wales for a weekend by the seaside.

Sunday morning aunt and I were drinking coffee while the children played in the garden. I stood by the window watching them and sipping from a china cup while I steadied my knees and prepared myself.

"So you are on your own this morning dear?"

The question released the tightness in my chest and I heard the story unfolding, silencing the noise of children's play, along with every other sound in the world. I tried to speak quietly but it still drowned every other noise. I wondered if I could be heard next door, or in the supermarket down the road. When the story was over I noticed that I still held my cup off its saucer. There was a pause. I stood looking out of the window and concentrated on replacing my cup as quietly as possible. This kept me calm. Finally my aunt addressed the hands she had folded in her lap.

"There is absolutely no question of my lending you money or supporting you in any way whatsoever. I am not married because my fiancé was killed in the First World War. When you give your word to someone as a promise for life you do not get halfway through and casually change your mind. I would have liked to have children too but the father they could have had was dead. I would strongly suggest that you reconsider ruining the lives of all those who love you and try to discover a sense of responsibility. Your bed is of your own choice. You must learn how to lie on it. Now dear, have you finished with your cup or would you like some more coffee? The biscuits are very nice. They're home made".

I waived the second cup of coffee. "I'm sorry if I have shocked you. I have to do this I'm afraid, one way or another. It will hurt in the short term but I have to start telling the truth. I know I haven't been doing that".

"I've got to go out so I must lock up. The truth is that you're selfish and don't deserve the family you have. ".

When later I told mother I reran the script for the morning and the preparation must have helped because she began to cry and it was the first time I can remember that I had confronted her and *she* had cried. Always it had been me. My mother said nothing but gave me £1000 to pay the deposit on my new home without a murmur of disapproval. It seemed to be a pivotal moment, as though she was finally accepting who I was. I drove home pleased with the outcome, but wishing I had not had to go down such a convoluted route to hide my own weakness. .

I moved with the children when their summer term finished. I calculated that by the time they returned for the next school year the new routine would have been established with minimum disruption. Then at the end of August my aunt had a stroke and was not expected to live. Between hospital visits I stayed with the children in her empty house. The old family house had passed to her, the unmarried daughter and I saw the excitement in my children that I remembered having when we moved to my paternal grandparent's old house. There was much rooting in wardrobes and cupboards for things they had never seen before, like pink, boned corsets with laces and rows of hooks. I rescued feather boas and jet beads from excited fingers and they chased each other with fox furs complete with head, feet and beady eyes.

Lying in the old fashioned featherbed, surrounded by the mahogany furniture, I tried to imagine the girl of 1917 and wondered if she had made love to her love before he was killed. Probably not. Love out of wedlock would be unthinkable for the owner of these white kid Sunday gloves with matching white leather prayer book. My aunt lived and worked all her life in the butcher's shop. She had been engaged to her cousin who was in the navy. They courted in the upstairs drawing room when he was on leave, the rest of the family discreetly remaining in the dining room downstairs.. What opportunity for sin? After his death she took responsibility for the shop and after her father died she kept on his two assistants and managed the whole business until the co-op bought her out and turned the block into a supermarket. She had lived out her retirement in a stolid square sensible house full of family treasure that was hoarded and polished and dusted daily, weekly, annually.

She died three days later. I arranged the funeral and afterwards mother and I ate a finger buffet and sipped sherry with friends from the church. When everyone had left I filled the dustbin with jam, and homemade vinegars and pickles made out of habit every autumn and now gathering dust and mould in cupboards and under the stairs with no one to know how long they had been there. There were apples in paper stored under the bed and a tray of pears ripening in the airing cupboard. Much later the solicitor called to inform me that I was a beneficiary in my aunt's will. The house and its contents were now mine.

"THE PATH OF DUTY IS THE
PATH TO GLORY."

Picture Postcard sent to Dora from Jack in 1917

I stayed in the house for a week not able to believe that it was mine and I was financially secure. In the large wardrobe in the main bedroom I found a hand made satin trousseaux embroidered D&J – Dora and Jack. Sheets, pillowcases, bias cut slips and nightdresses; laced and beautiful and never worn. In the drawer beside her bed were three letters addressed to her. One included a poem from Jack on board ship, loving and missing her. He thanked her for the woollen socks she had knitted and then wrote-

Well I remember how you said to me,
With quivering lovely lips, just as the train
Went out, Goodbye, You'll soon be back again"
And kissed me on the mouth. But I could see
Beneath your brave farewell, the misery
I shared with you, and in your eyes the pain
Of all the patient women who remain
Waiting at home, whilst we hold guard at sea.

The hardest lot is theirs, who wait in dread
For those they love, a dread they may not show.
With eyes grown heavy with the tears unshed.
Yet, dear, you were as proud to let me go
As I, in England's name, to strike a blow
To save the living – to avenge the dead

The second letter was from the war ministry and edged with black so no one could fail to know its contents as the postman delivered it. The third was from the ship's chaplain, expressing his sorrow at the tragedy and saying that Jack died quickly and bravely from a fever contracted from food poisoning. The ship had been in combat waters and sufficient medical aid was not available. All through the remaining years she had kept faith and then I announced my intention to throw away everything she had missed. Not only that, "...would you please give me the money to do it?"

I traced the careful embroidery with my finger and thought about the care and devotion that had prompted her to save all these things, carefully folded and treasured.. Nothing could replace what she had had. I thought about the early years of my music. The ability to play the piano and sing as well I could then had also been a treasure and now maybe I could somehow get it back. Maybe I could also discover why I felt like two different people. One was confident, in control and moving mountains as I had been today, and the other was unable to cope one to one with the simplest situation, like going to my mother for money instead of my aunt.

There seemed no balance, no easy ground between the two where I could live and be content. Presumably everything in one person has to be connected. I was determined to find the connection. Perhaps that could be her legacy to me – to give me not only the money, but the courage to use it to make a better life for me and for the children.

The inheritance made all the difference. Although owning two houses was not a long term option, my cottage could be comfortably furnished with selected items, while larger, more ornate furniture from the house in Wales was sold to provide carpets and fittings. I would keep my aunt's house as I disposed of the contents, then sell it and with the additional money from the sale of our family house, pay off my mortgage. I began to feel stronger and decided that the hysteria and inability to cope could be partly due to the stress of breaking up my marriage. As my self confidence returned maybe my voice would also improve and the problems would finally go away. Maybe I just needed to find 'me', know who I was.

The children were settled, loved the new house and saw their father regularly. In the long evenings with the children in bed I read or played the piano, or sat at the beautiful oak bureau doing my household accounts, much as Aunt Dora must have done her accounts for the butcher's shop. All completed I sat by the fire and returned again and again to the possible cause of the failure of my voice. I no longer mentioned it to anyone, guilty of my obsession But every time I opened my mouth to say anything at all, however trivial, someone spoke who was not me and that was impossible to ignore. Worse, to everyone around it *was* me, the only me anyone had known.

I sang through my students, producing and directing performances for schools with a cast of students from the education department. My involvement with the Arts Centre brought me into contact with professional productions and I was approached to sing Marcellina in Mozart's Marriage of Figaro, the gross buffoon who pursues Figaro with a bogus marriage contract. I had the experience, the stage craft and like all sad actors, a natural flair for comedy. More than anything I desperately wanted to be involved with the level of music making that I imagined would awaken something better in me. Rehearsals were over one month, the production ran for one week and I discovered in that time that I could no longer cope with music at this level.

Timed entrances and exits were the first nightmare. My body no longer moved in the natural rhythm of the music so a striding exit and a slammed door, timed to slam on the last orchestral chord, would find me halfway through the door at the crucial moment or I would be through the door and waiting for the slam. Neither would do in Mozart's precise musical choreography. The director despaired, the cast thought it funny and finally it had to be incorporated into the humour of the character because try as I might I could not get it right, something unthinkable ten years before.

I found myself standing offstage every rehearsal and every performance to listen to the countess sing her second aria and the applause that followed. How did that honeyed sound float from that slim, untroubled body, that face smile, those hands easily hang from those relaxed shoulders?

On the Friday as we left the theatre the car park a whirling white fog came down with snow underfoot. I switched on my headlights and moved gently forward to see someone wrapped and huddled crossing my path. It was the soprano who played the countess and suddenly a huge rage, frustration and pain engulfed me. I wanted to run her over and for a second I very nearly did. In panic I switched off engine and lights and she was gone. I sat terrified by myself and what was inside me. On the Saturday night I did not watch her sing, just sat in the dressing room while that velvet voice soared down to me over the intercom. I had to step down, out and away from music until I had tackled this devil. Was it my angel turned devil? Or was the angel as dead as my voice, my rhythm and my music?

No! I knew that somewhere in me my voice was actually OK, I knew from the work in the church I could sing hanging off a wall bar or doorway feet off the floor. I couldn't find the same voice standing up but I had to hang on to that slim hope of finding out why. I had seen the leaning tower of Pisa in the process of being rescued. Straps wrapped around the base and halfway up the tower were returning it gradually to some semblance of vertical. . Those straps were stabilised by blocks of concrete heavier than the tower itself. Was I a leaning tower providing my own straps and blocks of concrete to stop myself leaning any further?

I looked in the mirror but could see nothing, but then I didn't know what I was looking for. Had I stood against a panelled door for reference I would probably have seen what I was looking for but I could find nothing strange in my standing. Surely I must have been upright once. I ran about, played hockey, danced. I could remember dancing perfectly down rickety steps in some performance or other. How far back could I remember doing things like that?

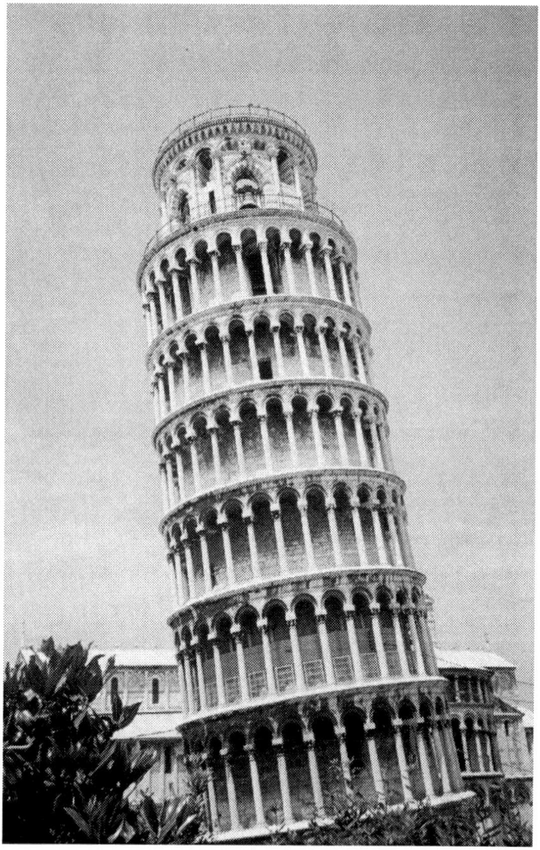

The Leaning Tower of Pisa

Chapter 9: Treating the Symptoms

I began to examine and re-examining that last college year and the summer after it for any clue. What had happened in my life in that year that might have knocked me off my feet? The only real trauma was that of being dragged off home at the end of my summer season. My mother's horror at my intention to stay and marry someone she considered totally unsuitable for her rising star. A mixture of fear and excitement rushed in. I was intrigued and wanted to reopen that chapter; close any unfinished business.

Now, apart from my singing I was secure in my own life. I was not young and failing any more. I was a self supporting single mother with my own house. I was a successful singing teacher. The young man who had turned my life upside down in one short summer would be married now of course, as I had been, with a family and a settled secure life but I still needed to clear my head of him. I went to the library and his unusual name was not hard to find. I wrote a letter to him at the family home, addressed "Mr and Mrs…." explaining that I was an old girlfriend that he had probably forgotten, I was happy and settled with two children and curious about him and his own family. I kept the letter in my pocket for a week opening, reading and rereading it. My better self, my angel knew what would happen and obviously tried to save all of us from the result, but the devil won. Late one night I went out and posted it

His wife never saw the letter. She was not interested in hand written letters in small envelopes. She was planning an expensive holiday so seized the glossy brochures He recognised but could not identify the writing so he slipped it into his pocket to take to work and open along with his business mail. He phoned but I was away staying with my mother. He wrote and the letter was on the mat when I returned.

"I have waited all these years to find you. When you left I crashed my mother's car- I did not want to live. I now have a life and a business and am rich, but not in the way we planned. We must talk about this".

It was twenty years almost to the day when I saw him again.

From the moment that I opened his letter I felt control slipping away.

I sat quietly at my desk in my cottage and wrote down all the achievements of the past six months. I was forty, financially secure and the children were happy and settled in their schools, with their friends and their lives. Considering what I had shaken up, our lives were good in spite of problems which, after all, were not problems to anyone but me. If I had complained about my unhappiness with my voice, my rhythm and that I thought I was falling over, any of my good friends would have worried about my sanity considering all I had going for me.

He came to see me, took me out to a splendid champagne dinner and offered to give up whatever he had achieved so far for us to be together, "if that is what you want". What I want? He had a wife and family who would be shattered by the break up of their home. I had already broken one, was I about to do it again, destroy more lives? I tried to think quietly about all the possible consequences but my head would not let me be quiet. It produced a constant flow of reasons for throwing away what I had and settling for the unknown. Friends advised but their caution only fuelled my resolve. If that was what I wanted.....Yes, the devil said that was what I wanted, so I embarked upon yet another change of course, with the devil's blessing.

I took the children to Suffolk for an experimental weekend and stayed by the sea. They loved the open space and the countryside. The weekend was like Christmas for them, all presents and spoiling. Who would not have wanted to go? Every apparently insurmountable problem I presented was solved either with money or influence, both of which he had in abundance.

The next six months roller-coastered into moving house, changing schools, leaving friends and colleagues, and finalizing my divorce settlement. All the practicalities were organized for me. I just had to maintain the manic energy to keep up and make sure everything and everybody was ready to move on time. But that was what I did best

. "My wife and children must not be deprived of any of the things which they have now. That would not be right. My business must therefore be secured while all the financial adjustments of a divorce are negotiated. It would be best if you bought yourself a house in the area and carried on earning your own living. You do have your aunt's house. You could sell that and buy a mortgage free property. It is absolutely vital for our future that I am not seen to support you in any way from the business. The bank may panic and that would be disastrous for all of us. As an employer I am responsible for nearly seventy people if you count the dependants. But, my darling, all that is just the practical side of our life, which I am good at and which need never concern you again. You deserve a break from all this. If someone can have the children, how would you like to go to Sweden for a few days?"

I had handed in my notice to all the organisations where I taught to begin a new life. I now went back to ask for my two days in London to be reinstated as I could travel there and earn enough in two days to keep myself and the children. I was impressed by the care he was showing for the lives of his employees. I was so lucky. At last I had made a decision myself that felt right.

Everything happened as if by magic. My aunt's house and my own were sold and a small temporary house was found that was a mortgage recovery. It required major repairs but it would be a good investment. I bought it outright. With loving care the wilderness became a garden and the house a comfortable home. We worked out a housekeeping budget based on my earnings with only a nominal rent from him and nothing else. This helped to secure a divorce settlement that bought his wife out of the business. It is apparently usual for two partners to make over 5% of the shares to their wives. By the return of her shares he became the major shareholder. Four years later his divorce was absolute and it was time to move on.

I had continued to work for the four years, agonizing over leaving my children overnight to work two days in London. His business was now secure and he was finally free It was time to put our finances together, enabling us to move out of this little house and on to the life we had planned. It was time to find our real family home.

"I've found it. I've found the house. It's got barns, a huge garden, a pond, everything. And it's old and beautiful. Take a day off and come and look"

"I can't promise to do that, but we could go one evening"

Later that week we sat in the local pub and talked money.

"Of course my capitol is tied up. We would have to use your house, which would cover half the purchase price. That would cut down mortgage repayments and give more to spend on renovation".

"I want to start with the kitchen. Great big kitchen table in the middle, copper pans, colour everywhere".

"It will be a lot of work. It's a big house and a big garden. How will you manage?"

"I can stop work now your finances are sorted out and put all my effort in here. We can get married and do this together. I could even run weekend courses for singing, now we have the space".

"Woa- woa- woa. If we are going to buy this place you will have to work a bit longer. We can't have it all, not all at once. The divorce has cost a lot of money. I had to give her everything she would have had if I'd stayed. I've given her the house and she can't be expected to work, she never has had to. Of course, if you hadn't gone twenty years ago, you would have had all that and this house too I dare say. Another drink?"

I sold my house and used the capitol to buy the big house with the big garden, which went into our joint names. He began to pay the mortgage on the rest. I gardened, decorated, made curtains and was blissfully happy. The gardener across the road, who could grow anything, taught me to grow vegetables, fruit and flowers. He took pity on my efforts, so obviously amateur but enthusiastic. He saw me out in all weathers struggling with sacks and barrows and bales to make a bed for the strawberries (is that why we call them strawberries?) so he more or less took me on as his apprentice. He taught me to make a hole for the leeks with a dibber, drop a leek in and fill the hole with water. I learned not to replant the thinnings of the carrots – this caused him to hold his sides and laugh, but he liked my willingness to struggle with the land and I like to watch him dig. His back fascinated me. He was so strong and upright and strode across the furrows of potatoes like a young man. Only when he turned back to you did you see his seventy years.

The outbuildings provided places to hang and climb. It was the church space once again without the walk through the dark graveyard. I began work to try to sing again. Two days a week I continued to train it to London to teach singing and inevitably I reported on my progress singing and hanging in the barn. Colleagues were both amused and fascinated and I was persuaded to arrange a couple of weekend courses. On the Saturday evening we had a concert. The village provided the audience, children from the village played in the concerts and although I never felt comfortable singing I made myself take part and this encouraged others who were similarly uncomfortable about singing. Through those concerts I began to see how many people would also give their eye teeth to be able to stand up and sing easily and comfortably. I was not the only one seeking a solution for an unsatisfactory voice. I broached the idea of developing this into regular voice workshops that would emphasize that singing was also a physical exercise.

"Maybe that's what I should be doing. Now I have this place and all the experience I have of struggle with my own voice maybe I can run some weekends for non singers. I never thought the people who came would enjoy themselves so much. Singing has been so traumatic for me for so long, but everyone just wanted the opportunity, said they had never had encouragement before, just total put down over their voices. The weekend gave them the opportunity to try to sing in a safe place with no destructive criticism. I had them hanging from the beams in the workshop and running round the field. Everyone was so different at the end of the weekend, so much happier. Maybe I could develop something important from this. What do you think?"

"I think you've enough to do looking after the children and this place without filling it up with other people".

"But they're not children any more. They are eighteen and twenty. They hardly need looking after. Most of the time they don't even live here and this is something I'm good at. I was trained in music and singing.. I would love to try this and we have an ideal place that is big and away from anything judgemental".

"This place is big because that is what you wanted. Just don't take on too much that's all".

I sat in the garden and thought about it. It always seemed that his priorities came first and his priority was always the business. I still hadn't the kitchen I wanted because when money was available outside maintenance was deemed to be more important. But when he had a large and thriving business why wasn't it possible to do both? I had carried on working to make the house possible but all I could see was investment pouring into his empire "for our future". Why was there never any money to spend on our lives? Why was I still working when he was a major shareholder in a very large business? It was time for me to make just a small stand. After all, it was my house too so I had a say in what it was used for. Actually at the current rate of repayment the greater part of the house belonged to me! So I decided to go ahead.

I advertised weekends for non singers and arranged accommodation in the village. I picked up clients on Fridays from the nearest main line station fifteen miles away. They stayed in the village but ate at the house. Two ladies from the village came to help and in no time they were making cakes for tea and encouraging their grandchildren to pay recorders in the concert. On those weekends the house filled with music and singing. We ran round the garden singing as we went, hung over the gates and swung from the beams in the barn. I knew that stretching and hanging had improved my voice. Now I knew it improved everyone's voice and gave voices to those who thought they had none. I was beginning to teach singing in quite a new way and in just two days some voices improved out of all recognition. However, not mine. It would be fine in the running, skipping and climbing, but not in the concert when I stood up to sing. But this was exciting and people enjoyed it so.

Unfortunately I made no money, try as I might. Each weekend someone would cancel for some reason or weather would suddenly descend, cancelling everything. I had not done anything like this before so my budget was often way out. But the weekends were so good for so many people. He began spending more and more time at work. Maybe all those people in the house, singing and filling the place with noise and themselves. Then one Sunday, instead of cutting the grass…

"It's a lovely day. We haven't been out for ages. Come on, I'll take you for a ride. We'll have tea out or a walk by the sea"

I skipped like a child. We walked by the sea in the sun. I watched the birds, felt the breeze and was content. I had also stood my ground, probably for the first time, and what had come out of it was not a mess, but something good. People had loved the courses, the home cooked food, finding the ability to sing. When he pulled me close under his arm to walk through an arch in a wall away from the sea I smiled my love up at him.

"I wanted you to see this. I've just bought it – my new business. Boats! There's a hole in the market for boats of this size. I've been very lucky, this premises almost fell into my lap. Of course it will be a struggle for a bit, money may be a bit tight, but in the long run….."

You lied to me today, nothing serious
Just half-truths, leaving something out,
Then speaking out, and found out.

I laughed and turned around to face you with it
So you could laugh and kiss me, tuck your face
Into my neck and say "you found me out…"
But then I saw your face and didn't.
There was a shadow on it I had seen before,
So then I knew you'd lied before
And would again.
I said "Oh really?"
Placing my voice box next to yours
I felt the velvet in your throat, the kid glove in the lung.
So often you have said "My Darling", with that voice.
I eased my stomach past you, tightened gut
For shelter of that special un-named place
So softened by your words of love.
How best survive?
Grow a hard shell, pull legs and feelers well inside and batten down
At every pretty word.

Chapter 10: And Yet Again ...

I don't really know what first made me embark on the dental work. Maybe I went for a filling or a check up and the dentist persuaded me that at my age it was time to think about the future of my teeth. I knew that I smiled only as far as the last visible tooth. There were teeth further back in my upper jaw but a wide smile exposed the space in between. In my twenties I had recurring toothache and could only tell the dentist "the pain is here". 'Here' was always a tooth and the tooth was duly removed. When removed the tooth was always found to be sound, yet they hurt like hell before they were pulled. Now I had a façade of six teeth to smile with and few molars to chew on.

"I could fit bridges to your upper arch because you have teeth either side of the space. It would widen your smile and give you more confidence."

I booked a series of appointments which would include fitting bridges to spaces left by extractions in my twenties. When the dentist said they would cost £600 I got a kick out of agreeing. I was feeling pretty sore about yet more business investment and this would be just for me. He could hardly tell the dentist he couldn't afford his wife's teeth. A month later the bridges were fitted To settle the account I said, "Send it to the business address", and I made two or three attempts to do this before a drunken phrase struggled out along with some dribbling. My tongue did not seem to belong to me. "Don't get stopped on the way home" she laughed. I drove home feeling I could no longer talk.

At home I wanted to keep stretching my jaw wide open. My cheeks did not seem wide enough or high enough to accommodate the extra teeth, two on the left one on the right in the upper jaw. What better way of stretching the face than having a good sing. I went into the music room and began. For the first few minutes I repeatedly bit the side of my tongue. I had noticed this when driving home. Of course, the tongue must usually spill sideways into the spaces that had now been filled. I attempted to pull it back out of the way and my voice suddenly changed. It was a shock and I stopped singing. When I sang again I could not do so for coughing deep down in my throat. Each change of pitch tickled and choked me, stopping the sound. I was fascinated and continued to sing/cough until the familiar tyres on gravel sounded an hour later.

"I have told the dentist to send the bill to you as you have the cheque book at the moment"

My tongue seemed to have taken up the position I had been pulling it into while trying to sing without coughing. No more biting, just resting between the new teeth and filling the back of my mouth. It was a very strange feeling but quite comfortable. In fact my voice felt much stronger and more resonant.

"I meant to ring the bank and tell them that they haven't sent a cheque book here for ages. You must also be running out of cheques by now"

I never questioned him about money. I always waited to be told. I listened to myself in admiration as I pursued the matter.

"I haven't had to write a cheque for some time so I haven't mentioned it before. Why do you think they have not sent it?"

"How should I know? I'll pay when I get the bill like I always do".

Shortly afterwards mother died, leaving me the first money of my own that I had seen for some time. I put it into a separate account.

Whatever had kicked off in me went from bad to worse. I had been taken on regular business trips abroad. These were our holidays. The next trip was to the Greek Islands, courtesy of some dependant company or other. As we checked into the Hotel energy bubbled inside me that would not be quiet. The first hospitality evening was a fancy dress party and I went as a wild woman dressed in a sack, with false fangs and a crazy wig.

Later, on the way to the ladies, I passed the Hotel lounge where families watched a huge TV. Children sat at every table fidgeting and bored while parents downed the drinks and ignored them. Passing the lounge on the way back I leapt inside the door and interrupted the TV programme with a Neolithic howl that brought every child to its feet and running after me.

This was in no way planned, it just seemed the thing to do on the spur of the moment, but oh the joy of doing something mad, fun and funny. The Greek Hotel staff, equally bored at the reception, on the door or serving at the bar joined in the game as I ran and the children chased me all over the Hotel. To get back to the party, like the pied piper I led the running children back into the TV lounge. As I jumped over a stool a boy caught up with me and hooked my legs from under me. Momentarily I crashed to the floor and while parents seized their children I got up and escaped into the private hospitality room where we had had dinner.

"I wondered where you'd gone. I was about to come looking for you"

Dinner was at coffee and liqueurs. When we rose to leave the tables I found I could not stand on my right foot. Later that night a doctor was summoned and the story was out. I had broken a small bone in my ankle. No hospitalisation, but strapping and limited mobility. At breakfast next morning my new friends smiled and chatted, the hotel staff in the dining room filled my cup the moment it was empty and the head waiter winked at me as we entered the dining room as though we had spent the night together.

The business party were half bemused, half embarrassed.

"Your good lady seems to be quite a star this morning, eh?"

But all these jolly faces were eclipsed by the darkness and threat of the anger which positively incinerated my husband's eyebrows; a single thick welded line above rock like features. He spoke not a word, nor had done since the doctor had left at 3 am. Well, that is not a word to me. He said things that related to me about making tea and having a shower – that sort of thing - but he addressed all this to the curtains, or the tea bag, or the light fitting on the opposite wall.

Finally, at the end of breakfast, he spoke to the orange peel left on the plate.

"We will walk down to the beach, if you can make it that far"

Did I dare not?

"I feel we have some things to discuss"

We walked down to the beach, he supporting me through the pool area where the group were on the third round of drinks and then he let go as if he could not bear to touch me. We sat on a rock facing the sea and the "discussion" began.

"I have taken you half way round the world, shown you a life which you would never have been able to afford. This is the last time I will take you anywhere. Do not apologise or try in any way to even talk about it. You are well aware by now that once I have made my mind up about something I do not change it. I would have thought that you would have been grateful for this second chance to have a proper life. I offered you the best twenty years ago. You did not know how to behave then and that has not changed. I have to admit that all my friends warned me. My wife at least knew how to behave. You have humiliated me. The people we are with are important clients. There are business connections here worth a lot of money. You don't live in the real world......"

on and on he went while I sat and watched the sailboarders tip into the water and climb purposefully back on to catch the wind and speed off across the waves.

I would not have caused this problem a few months before. I would have thought about it, but the thought would have remained in my head. I would have gone back to the dining room with my imagination running riot. Like Billy Liar I would have sat smiling at the host and cooling my anger and frustration by fantasizing him into a long slow death, probably brought about by the bored children in the next room. Somehow a connection had been forged between that imagination and the rest of me. To my amazement another connecting rod suddenly rammed home and my voice and brain began to work together in a steady, resonant and quietly determined way

"I really enjoyed running and playing with those kids. Everyone enjoyed it except you and all those boring businessmen and their boring wives who are too busy maintaining their market profile to enjoy themselves. Your anger is about what they might think and what they may do to your business bottom line as a result. I can't be like that. I can't think like that. There's got to be a better way to enjoy yourself"

While this was going on I did notice that my tongue was reared up in the roof of my mouth and hitting those new bridges with every measured, resonantvowel.

He suddenly became very angry and stood up. He was already a big man but he looked much bigger. The expression on his face, no the expression on the whole of him told me he was out of control. I have always had a reputation for being able to deal with drunks, dogs and children. I learned it being in front of a summer audiences on wet Wednesday afternoons when parents on holiday leave the children in the theatre and go back to the hotel for peace and sex. There is nothing between you and a couple of hundred ravening children except a bad comedian and a few balloons. Or maybe it was school teaching. Anyway I did the same as with all other hostile attackers. I stayed exactly where I was and waited for him to make the next move.

"I gave up my wife and family for you. I never took her to the places I have taken you, introduced her to my business friends. She would have loved to go with me, sit at the top table. Look at the presents you've had because of targets I've reached. The cut glass, the perfume, the leather cases. You didn't say "No" to all that did you? Well you will now. I shall make sure that none of it comes your way again. You are out!"

And with that he strode away, leaving me to get back to the Hotel as best I could. At 5.30 he came in from the Taverna.

"We need to get ready. We have to be downstairs at 6.30"

"I assumed you would go without me".

"You will complete this trip and not embarrass me further. The arrangement we discussed begins as soon as we get home."

We went down in the lift without a word and joined the glamorous gathering. He laughed and joked about my escapade the previous night, arm around my shoulders, apparently proud of the attention I had brought us and as amused as everyone else.

"You must bring her to Birmingham next time you visit us. We could do with someone lively around. We're actually thinking of a playground promotion next year in which we involve local schools – introduce our temporary building units"

They never stop – any of them.

Once home there was a period of neutrality when it appeared that my behaviour had been forgiven. I *had* kept the presents, I *had* been taken all over the world and he *had* every cause to believe I was ungrateful and unworldly. From where he stood the view was different, the world was a market and money was the only currency. So I cooked and I gardened and I tried. I had a log fire and a scotch waiting for the tyres on gravel, the key in the door. I cooked the dinner, arranged the table, opened the wine and waited but the gravel did not crunch. He did not come. I finished the wine by the fire and rang his private number at work, but he was not there. I opened the whisky.

He returned at 2am, noted the empty wine and half empty whisky bottle and went to bed, leaving me asleep on the mat before the now dead fire. I woke later to see his car in the drive and then discover him tucked up in bed. I crept in, cold and cowed by events, knowing that a war was beginning that I may not win. This was a formidable enemy. The warring factions were his reasonable and functional world against what was bubbling intermittently in me. If only I could access the connecting rods that seemed to focus me. If not I may die a casualty of it.

He was ready to go to work early, full of pleasantries and I resisted the desire to ask him where he had been. However, I did ask him what time he would be in to dinner.

"I don't know. I'll ring you. I'm very busy at the moment. By the way, your car is due for service. I'll take it in this morning. It may need major work"

"What will I do for transport?"

My voice betrayed panic. We lived miles from habitation.

"My car will be here till I can sort something out"

Yes, but not the keys I discovered later. I cycled to the nearest town primarily to prove to myself I was not under a control I did not accept. Where had this fight back come from? On return I felt so good I could have run around the garden beating my chest and hollering. Instead I sang everything I knew and played the piano very loudly. I also finished the rest of the whisky.

I woke at 5 am, knowing that he had a very important meeting in the Midlands. A large shiny car stood outside ready for the occasion. He would wake at 6am with the alarm, dress and leave by 6.30. I tiptoed downstairs, lifted his car keys from the hook in the kitchen and threw them as far down the garden as I could. I then went back to bed and lay waiting for the alarm. I wasn't particularly afraid of the outcome of what I had done, but quite afraid of what had made me do it. What relief it had been to throw the keys as hard as I could and how after that moment I stood, watching the early sun and listening to the birds before I went back to bed.

"I threw them down the garden".

There was no satisfaction for me in having him hunt for them. Anyway he always hung them in the same place, so his first question was not

"Have you seen my keys?"

But

"What have you done with my keys? "You did WHAT?"

"You took my car without any warning or asking me if it was OK. I've done the same. I want to be consulted about things that are to do with me. You now feel like I felt yesterday morning"

Where had I found the courage to stand up to him? Where had it come from? In the years we had been together he had little by little – softly, softly, catchee monkey, taken control of every facet of my life. He had not been happy in his own marriage and I fulfilled his wildest expectations. Not only had I lost all personal confidence I needed to nurture and protect my children. I was a wounded lioness with cubs. That gave him a lever. But the best was trailing behind me as I fell. My own house that he could comfortably move to and a thunderous desire to please. I fell out of my life and he caught me, collecting everything else on the way.

The mind is a wonderful thing. As I stood in the kitchen waiting for punishment it had done a complete reappraisal of my situation. But where had this present intelligent mind been when he was taking control of all this? I could see it now. Why could I not see it when it was happening?

It took him an hour to produce another car and return to plan A. During that hour the only things said were,

"You have a serious problem that has to be faced. You are not quite right in the head and you need help to get you back into the normal world. You need some discipline. You think that everything comes to you as a right. You don't want to make any effort, just have all this and please yourself. Your children have the same problem. None of you have any gratitude for living in this big house and having all the advantages I have given you."

After he left the strong and the weak in me pitched into each other. I felt fingers of fear in my stomach wanting to retrieve my steps, make everything right again. He had done so much for me to move me here – dealt with the solicitors, organised the furniture removal, helped me to clear and pack up the house, kept me out of the way of the disapproval of his local business associates, friends and family.

"Wait!"

said the strong.

"Everyone saw me as a fortune hunter who had pushed herself into his life. He told no one that I had funded the move, bought my own house and earned my own living for most of the years we had been together. I had paid my way into this big house. He had taken advantage of me, the weak and compliant me".

"But I had been in a hopeless mess", I argued

"and he came in with his business head and what would I have done if he hadn't? If he took it all from me I let him. I leaned gratefully on him and let him take complete control of my life because I had none. Now I was questioning my gratitude and his motives but my behaviour *was* irrational and he was right about that. One minute I was washing his hair in the bath and playing him music, the next I was going out of my way to be confrontational".

He began to avoid this trouble by not coming home. I wandered the empty house and garden knowing I may have to leave yet again as there were no answers to any of my questions here. He had always had two lives, private and corporate and he merely had to step entirely into his work to render me impotent. Both children now had partners and their own homes. I replaced a stray garden fork in the shed and moved my gardening shoes onto the shelf. They stood heel to heel and I idly took one of them away. The other leaned alarmingly, threatening to fall over. I had become so angry with that Alexander Teacher when he pointed this out to me so many year ago. What if I stepped out and went back to study, not when I had time but as a committed student. My inheritance could pay the course fees. The last time I had felt close to discovering anything about myself had been when my shoes fell over in the kitchen and I knew now that instead of listening to the alarm bells I had run for cover. I would become a full time student, go away and study the Alexander Technique.

I needed an opportunity to discuss this and it came sooner than I planned. I ran out of cheques before my new chequebook came and phoned the bank.

"It was sent out ..."

So I waited, then went to the bank and asked to see the manager. I gave my name and repeated my request. I had never been to the bank before in my own right, only with my husband, who was one of their biggest customers.

"I have not received my cheque book. Could it have been sent somewhere else?" (Who put that question in my head?)

The manager scuttled off and returned looking suitably embarrassed.

"We have instruction to send all banking correspondence to the business address. We have a signed mandate ..."

"Who signed it? This is a joint account. How can you change joint account instructions without joint signatures?"

"We understood that your husband had signed on both your accounts...."

He suddenly saw immediate danger fill the whole office and threaten to burn down his life.

"... Er ... I could issue you a temporary cheque book while we sort out the problem ..."

"Thank you that will do nicely".

I did not have to ask him to come home. He came through the door like a musk ox with a bee up its nose.

"You have been to the bank to cause trouble".

Fortunately I appeared to have my strong bit working.

"I have been to the bank to discover what arrangements have been made to prevent my access to my money".

"YOUR money".

"Well I mean our money".

"Oh no that's not what you said.. YOUR money, that's what you said. You have been to the bank to make sure that you can spend, spend, spend as you like. Did you tell the manager you go through cheque books like confetti? No of course not. You told him your wicked husband deprived you of everything. Look at the car you drive, the coat on your back. Do you look deprived? Most women would give their eye teeth for such depriving".

"You forged my signature, you lied".

"I never lie. I said it was easier for me to take care of the money because that is what I did best. You had more important skills"

I did not even feel angry - pointless to pursue the definition of a lie. Whatever I said he would merely open up the jar, put in the stick and stir this little beetle around, tormenting it for as long as he wished. That had to stop now.

"I'm going away".

"Go where you like".

"I'm going to the Lake District. I shall take a cottage and study. I've got to get away from you and the way I've begun to behave. I need to break this pattern. I need to find out what sets it up".

"And what are you going to do for money? Where's this dream cottage coming from? Am I to be told who's paying for it? What his name is?"

"I have the money for my fees. *We* are paying to rent me a cottage out of our joint account because you said I needed help and this is the help I need".

Got him!

You went tonight to someone else's arms.
I heard you plan it on the phone. Your voice
Was tender as you said "Hello, it's me"
You did not give your name. She knew.
I also knew, although I only heard you mutter your assent, say
"Those arrangements which you put to me this morning.
It's OK I can make it. Go ahead. Make the reservation".
You could have phoned from work.
You waited all the day to make that phone call
Until you could be sure that I would hear.
You could have phoned at any time, but you needed
To have me there to hear you, in case a little chink
Remained between my armour and myself;

I watched you go. Held myself together easily;
Made up the fire and fed the cat.
I found a book I wanted to explore. I read,
And as I read a world unfolded I'd not known before.
When you returned, I did not even hear you close the door

I made the mistake of turning my back to walk away. That broke the spell and the flying kick aimed at my bottom caught me squarely under the bum and laid me flat. Survival became paramount. I rolled onto my feet and held onto the fireplace, facing him squarely and still as I would have a vicious dog. He was white and his huge hands were in fists. If he hit me now he would kill me. However I could now see from his face that he was more frightened than I was at what he had just done.

"I'm sorry. I had no right to demand anything. But I do have to go, you can see that. This cannot go on and it's getting worse. I would like to study and I do have to live somewhere. I want to find out what is wrong with me and put it right. That will benefit everyone".

He shouted some more things about lack of responsibility and slapped me around. I took it without retaliating because now he was shouting and blustering and it was to frighten me and save face. Eventually I got away to the bathroom where I locked the door and remained until I heard him go to bed and all the lights were off. I then locked myself in a back bedroom and returned to the kitchen the next morning when the wheels had crunched out of the drive. I packed my things, and left.

One week later I was walking the hills at the back of Kendal with a sheaf of estate agent information, looking for somewhere to spend the winter. A letter written on business paper informed me of his decision to pay for accommodation for me for one year "as that is what you want". I had enrolled locally on a full time course to study The Alexander Technique.

So nothing would ever be easy. That was the message. Don't run, don't hide, don't look for someone to look after you. You will not escape the programme for it is set. It was set way back and someday you will discover when that was and what set it.

He has paid for a year but it will take much longer than that and you may never go home again.

I've never been out here with no one to go back to,
I can't remember when I pleased myself-
When to have supper, what to have.
You didn't like sweet things.
Preferred meat spiced, or fish grilled;
'Specially herrings. I don't buy them now.
How is the house I wonder?
Have you taken down the plain matt tiles
Put mirror tiles in the bathroom?
"To give it space" you said
But space alone is cold I know.
I made space warm for you and washed your hair
On Saturdays when you had closed the week.
You took the house "To clean it up" you said
"To tidy up your slovenly ways"
I took your offer, left, and went away.
I walked the hills, recovered; dragged the old life
Out from every toenail.
Forgot the curtains, cushions, key that would not turn,
The tree I planted and the rose I smelled.
I have a whole life stretching out before me.
Children are settled, choice unlimited. I'm struggling
With the concept of having my own life.
Maybe you do the same.
How sensible we have become,
But how we loved ... herrings ..... Saturdays.

Chapter 11: The Alexander School

My life was yesterday and now is not my life.
Yesterday I understood the now, remembered well
The up and down of hurry here and there,
The comfortable programme holding thus-, releasing thus-,
That life has gone, the people gone, the music gone,
The sun, air, blood of yesterday all stopped,
Cut through as clean as splitting slate
To fall in pieces on the floor.
I gently carry this new now into my heart, breasts, sides,
Moving inside with wonder, discovering new life in every moment.
Every sight, touch, sound and smell of it.

I stood looking out of the window and counted my toes as the teacher pressed each one in turn from the big toe out. I came confidently to 'this little piggy had none' and waited for her to press the 'wee-wee-wee-all the way home' while watching the surrounding hills turn pink in the setting sun. "You don't seem to recognise your little toes. I have been pressing them for ages with no response". Another area of me I had given up, lost and left for dead. How much of me had died? The teacher moved on to another pair of feet.

Most of the first term consisted of stepping out of the usual pattern of one's life and allowing mind and body to have the space and time to reflect. After the first day of discussion over timetables and book lists there began a daily routine of regular lying on the floor and "letting go". I spent all this time asleep. I also slept through anatomy, Alexander work, conversations, lunch, evenings in the pub, a rousing Irish pipe band at the folk club and in my bed all night, every night.

The one session I could not sleep through was meditation. We all sat in a circle for twenty minutes every morning to empty the mind and body of the tensions and distractions we all carry around with us, except that there was absolutely no way that I could sit or kneel, no matter how many cushions, that was not complete agony. After a very short time my right hip began to develop what could only be described as toothache. Like toothache it began as a small white hot centre and then spread until it engulfed me.

I would then shift the weight load by crossing my legs the other way; stretching one leg out in front or tucking more cushions under the crook of my knees. The pain would then radiate from a new centre. I began to actually meditate on my pain, closing my eyes and visualising the centre of it in the black in front of me. This way I managed to last out for the twenty minutes – just, but although I showed nothing of it except for the occasional shift of position, tears always escaped down my face for at least the last five minutes.

I was surprised at how readily I slipped into this way of coping. By the end of the first week I merely knelt and waited for the pain to come and then began to concentrate on it. At the end of the session other students put their arms around me and envied my ability to "let go of all my stuff". They would never believe that it was just sheer physical pain and absolutely no "stuff" had let go anywhere.

Yet what happened in the bathroom, the concert where I sang out of tune, the darkened church where I hung? Was that not a letting go? Or was it collapse, which was not quite the same thing? Letting go was voluntary, collapse was when you just couldn't hold yourself up any longer. But why I was holding myself up? Why wasn't I strong enough to just stand there on two feet and respond reasonably to whatever came?

"You never stand still. You don't sit still either. This is indication that you are not grounded".

"Grounded?"

"Your weight should travel down your spine, divide in your hips, be evenly distributed down the legs, into the feet and into the earth. You are holding all this weight in the area of your pelvis as if you were responsible for carrying the load. You don't allow that weight to be divided between the legs, travel equally down the legs and be transferred onto the ground. That is what is meant by a state of natural balance; equal weight on two free and flexible legs. You are always working against this system and holding yourself up with all of the muscles you can access to do it. Of course this is impossible, your body is not designed this way so you are struggling against falling over all the time. This would account for your manic and unstable behaviour"

I thought hard and long about the picture of me holding a great weight in my abdomen, but my body failed to understand any of it. I had no sensation of carrying any weight anywhere and when I tap danced, which I frequently did rather badly for fun, I could feel my heels and toes clattering the floor with what seemed to be great weight.

By the end of first term tutorial my body was so confused that I failed to understand one simple instruction without seizing up and becoming rooted to the spot. I could not explain the panic I felt at having a teacher unlock my knees by moving them slightly while I stood looking out of the window of the school and across the town roofs. I would tense my whole body and grab the floor with my feet for protection – against what?

"I want you to take this balance board home with you at Christmas and teach yourself how to stand on it. When you can stand on this with your whole weight distributed evenly over two feet I believe you may be able to sing".

Christmas. What was I to do about Christmas? For all of my life Christmas had been family and friends; presents and a tree. Boxing Day was lunch for anyone wanting to come; turkey and pork pies; trifle and stories. What would I do? Where would I go?

And what about the children? O come on, stop calling them the children! They have their own partners, lives and houses. They were even married now. The past three years had been a succession of weddings in their community of friends. They were now away and safe from the mess of divided families; the jealousies, the in-fighting, the emotional blackmail; at least you hoped. Sometimes the in-fighting was easier to cope with than the utter reasonableness with which one attempted to protect the children, as if children did not understand passion and desire and longing and disempowerment and the hate you had for someone who stole your favourite thing and never gave it back.

I got the wedding photographs today
All leather bound. The video came last week.
They couldn't have had a better church,
The porch just fit the family.
And then a perfect distance from the door
There was a marble slab ideal to mount the tripod.
We had to move an urn, with flowers, but put it back again
When he had captured every moment, every guest
That was related.

Forty six had come from Susan's side,
And we have lovely groups.
That's Sue and John and me with Clive - No -
That's not Sue's father, he's in later with his friend.
(I think she's very nice).
Clive and I have been together seven months.
That's Sally, John, and that's John's dad, such fun
And that's his second wife. John's mum was there
But wouldn't stand beside his dad, so she's in later.
I don't think she enjoyed herself at all. She's in between
A very long affair and starting a new job. Oh, there she is-
She never really smiled - so selfish, to spoil it for the happy couple.
There we are with all the family. The colours go so very well together;
If they had picked their outfits so they matched
They couldn't have done it better. Such lovely photographs -
Weddings are such fun, and then you get all this to keep
And look at as you both grow old together ...

I decided to post presents and cards to the two households, explain my problem and promise to see them early in the New Year. I would then stay in the cottage, shut the door, get on this balance board and make Christmas go away.

The end of the term was December 21st. I watched everyone drive away from the school and I walked purposefully up the fell side and away from the road to take the long route to the cottage, get there late and creep into my bed. It was dark in the lane and I was frightened. I wanted someone there to talk to as I walked. There had always been someone to want and need me. Now I felt as though I could walk across the edge of the hill into oblivion and everything would just go on without me.

"Now that's not true. Husband went to work, children to school, everyone was always going out of your life and leaving you alone. You enjoyed being alone. You walked the marshes, sewed, gardened, always on your own. When you really look at it you were just a little wooden top spinning in the middle of all these other people who came and went. Well that's the end of that persona. The children no longer need it and no one else is entitled to it. Now *I* am going to be one of the movers, the 'go-and–come-backers'. I now have a purpose, a direction to go in. Someone else can be the piggy in the middle..."

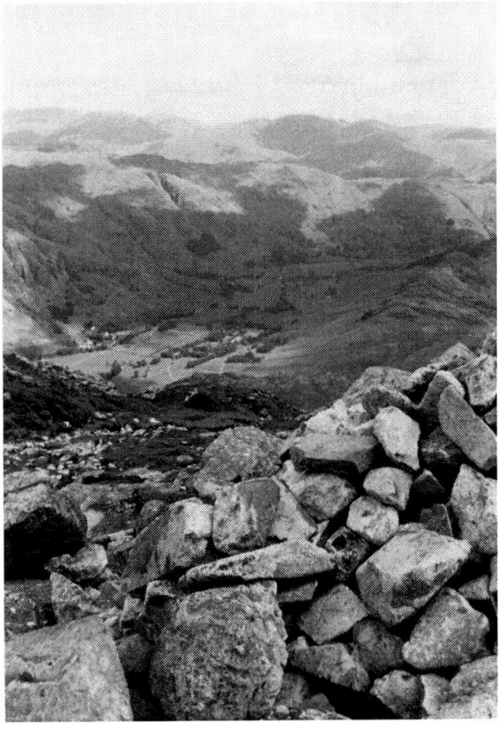

The Lake District

I was walking faster and faster, as though afraid of what was behind. My feet pounded the path and I could feel the tension in my legs. I stopped, to realise that I was now talking angrily out loud to the quiet night and the sheep.

"Oh please I can't be alone at Christmas, I just can't bear it-can't cope with it. I must have someone to love, to care for, someone who *W-A-N-T-S* me. A-a-a-ah-h-h-h-h ... " Vowels to the empty air. I reached out with my arms to the stars and howled them out of my stomach where the pain was beginning. I bent my knees to give me purchase, splayed my fingers to touch more sky and sang with the terrible singing I still endured so that the little mounds on the surrounding slopes scattered and disappeared.

After that I was able to cry. I could cry for the home I knew I had lost, for the husband I loved and could not cope with and who could not cope with me. For the children I missed and who were heartily sick of a mother who made scenes and drank too much and pursued grandiose schemes with a manic tunnel vision worthy of the Third Reich. Finally and most desperately I cried for the singing I hated now and loved once, but not for me. I could not cry for me.

I started to run as fast as I could in the dark, forcing my concentration back onto staying on this barely visible path until I finally blundered into a wall where the path turned. It stopped my run and my breath and I stood gripping the top stones, pulling the softness of my body against the hardness of the wall.

The wind cut in. I pulled my coat around me.
I had come to walk the fell, to look for newborn lambs;
Watch the trees whip and sway, the clouds scud.
But the wind cut in, into my neck, my face,
Sucked at my gut, razored my skin, my breath-
I cried out with the pain of it and tucked my chin
Into my coat, wrapped face up with my scarf-
Tightened my gut and squeezed myself in safe-
Safe from the wind.
It could not reach me now.
But neither could I see the lambs, the clouds, the fell,
The trees, or even now the path before me.
I stood still, holding myself tight together,

Safe from moving forward, reaching out.
All stopped, but I was safe.
I opened wide my eyes, let go my gut,
Smiled with my face and saw the lambs, the trees, the clouds.
The wind cut in, but I walked on,
Careless of the little pain of it.

I unpacked the balance board. It was a plain piece of board with a separate roller. You balanced the board on the roller, a foot either side. I put the board against a kitchen unit and held onto its surface to get on. Standing on it with my two legs adjusting to keep me in the middle was a wonderful feeling. I felt light as a dancer. I placed the board the other side of the kitchen so that I could do the same thing but look out of the window down the lane and I began to enjoy just playing with this thing. Part of the game was to take away my hands from the kitchen surface and put then on top of my head. But I only managed that with one hand at a time. That night my legs ached so much that I had to lie, instead of sit, on the sofa. Curious.

The next day I decided to begin work in earnest. The Director wanted me to be able to stand on the board by the beginning of the next term and he did not say anything about holding on. I placed the roller under the middle and put one foot on the end in contact with the floor. Then I put the other foot on the end which was in the air but kept all weight on the other foot. Somehow the board must come level by transferring half the weight. I tentatively began to transfer my weight to bring the contact end off the floor. As I felt the board lift just a little and

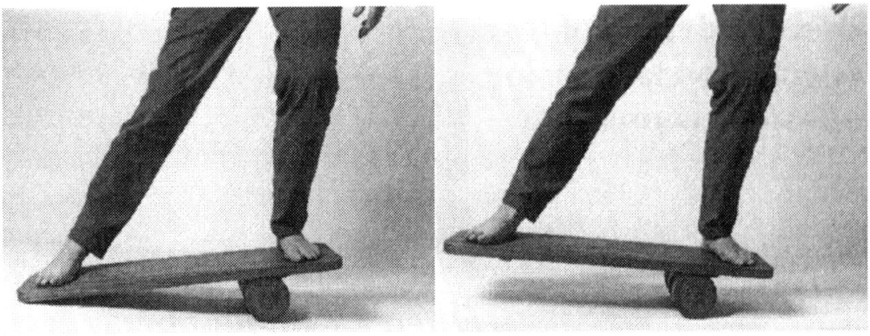

then return I went into a panic that stood sweat out on my forehead and clamped my fingers in a fist. I put the board away.

The next morning I began earlier and by the end of the day I could stand on the board without holding on. It was still very difficult but I could do it and I could sing a song before I fell off. I was so pleased with myself that I decided to pack up and go home. The New Year was about to begin and maybe all I had required was time to reflect, to recover myself. I missed home so much. We had both had time to rethink and friends had always insisted I was missing the real reasons for my behaviour.

"It's your age. Not everyone has hot flushes"

"A changing time in the family, children leaving home, you are bound to feel it..."

"Two marriages – most people have a job to deal with one..."

All the way home I felt strong and happy. I sang everything I knew and sometimes even thought that I sounded and felt better. The familiar countryside crept into view and I pulled into the drive. There were lights in the house and two cars outside, his and a smaller one. From my car I saw the neat black shoes beyond the chair with its back to me; one slim stockinged leg. Life had moved on here too and I knew I could never go back. Through my rear mirror I saw someone close the curtains as I pulled away. While I drove back to the cottage I had five hours to reflect that with my second marriage finally over and the children in their own lives there was no one dependant on me, I was responsible only for myself. So far that information had only been in my head.

I had been playing with the idea of recovery. Losing my singing had been critical for me because I was singer and performer. Of course it would be critical for me and ruin my life but I was beginning to see that having a voice problem might affect you even if you were not a singer and a performer. If my balance problem had caused my voice problem because balance and voice were connected that could mean that anyone with a balance problem could have a voice problem. After my singing had disappeared it was my speech and its affect on my relationships with other people that had created bigger life problems, the divorces, the inability to hold my own corner, the lack of confidence. My voice seemed to be suffering from the same kind of panic and dysfunction as my unbalanced body and my erratic brain.. Having a voice problem was a bigger issue than even I had imagined.

I returned to my cottage, my balance board and my walks on the fell. I had two more years of training but only three more months before the tourist season would claim the cottage and I would have to move out.

Look at you!
When will you start caring for yourself?
You had such wonderful ideas.
You broke the family up.
"To find yourself" you said.
You chose to be alone!
So look at you!
What changes have you made?

That woman, a casual friend who similarly screwed her life up.
There you were cooking her Sunday lunch.
“Taking her out of herself” you said.
You did this for your daughter when she was sixteen
And had that boy, or rather he had her…
That woman looks terrific now, she sucked it all from you.
You look awful, old and tired,
And still have much to do.
You have to stop the shoring up
Which you have done for thirty years!
If you really want to start again, to find yourself
And have a life for YOU -
For Chrissake learn to nourish YOU
For you’re the one who needs it most.
Stop getting eaten up
By those who claim to have no strength
To carry coal and make the fire that cooks the food
They ably carry to their mouths!

Chapter 12: Out of the Dark

The money my mother left me should have covered the course and some more besides, but it was running out. Inflation had increased the school fees and until the divorce settlement was finalised I had very little money. He could afford 'Rottweiler' solicitors so the account allowed to me on my credit card was minimal and any visit to a cash point was Russian Roulette. The Director of the Course encouraged me to teach at the school to supplement my allowance and allowed me to use an attic room where I had a bedroll, my sleeping bag and my books. The school facilities included a shower room and a kitchen so I had lived there since the contract ended on the cottage. Now an orthodontist from the local hospital became a pupil. Inevitably one day the conversation moved from what I did to what she did.

"I mostly fit appliances to straighten children's teeth"

"Why don't they have straight teeth to begin with?"

"Some children have narrow faces and there are just too many teeth for their mouths. Then the front ones may protrude, which is not very attractive, or the teeth just turn sideways and crowd. I take some out to make room for the others and then fit an appliance that pulls the other teeth into an attractive smile." I was fascinated.

"What does this appliance look like?"

Some lessons later she turned up with a little pink box containing a pink plastic shape that fit up into the roof of the mouth to secure the wire that wrapt around the arch of the upper teeth.

"How do they manage at school with this thing in their mouth?"

"They seem to cope".

"What does one of these things do to the voice?"

"I have no idea. It's not an issue".

"Who has worn one of these appliances who can judge whether it is an issue for them?"

"To my knowledge, no one".

"What if you made me an appliance? I could then give you that information".

"It's difficult to make an appliance that is neutral. You see everything that you put in a mouth promotes a reaction. It might move your teeth".

"At my age?"

"At any age. Teeth move very easily. I've never had to wear an appliance myself but the whole mouth area is very sensitive and we do know there is an immediate response to any intrusion. We don't know what that would be in your case".

I was intrigued with the idea that my teeth could be moved around at 50 and wanted something in my mouth to find out what would happen. She gave me an appointment at the hospital where she worked and took an impression to make me an appliance. The wires formed hooks around two side teeth to keep it in place and a further wire traced the outside arch of my upper front teeth. It was fitted one afternoon after school.

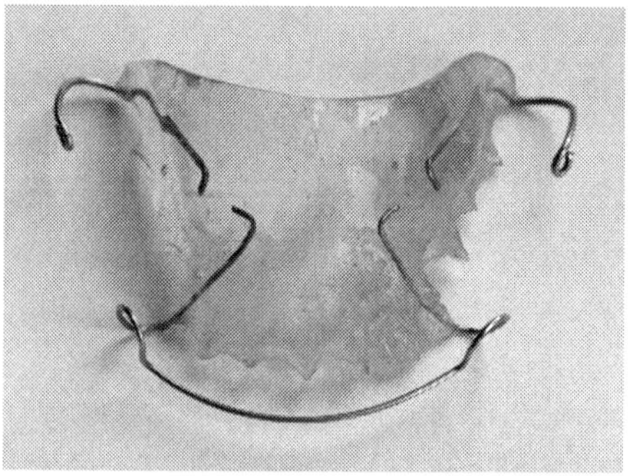

The 'neutral' appliance

As soon as it had been fitted I read some poems and sang into a tape recorder, all with hilarious consequences. My tongue could not cope with the reduction in space of the roof of my mouth so all consonants lost their precision and I sounded very drunk. The plan was to wait for half an hour and then repeat the poems and the singing to discover how I was beginning to accommodate for the appliance. This was a novel idea to me; that my body would accommodate for the speech problem; that my tongue and throat would change their actions so that I could speak and sing sounding 'normal'. However, if teeth can move, anything is possible. A further test was to drink a cup of coffee and eat a biscuit. I dribbled the coffee and could not even consider the biscuit. I began to feel that this was no longer funny, that I wanted to get away and learn how to cope with it alone. More than anything in the world I wanted to take it out and throw it away.

Half an hour later, when I repeated the poems on the tape I could speak more clearly, but I daren't try to sing. I was too close to crying. The orthodontist admitted that it was the first time she had spent so long with anyone after having fitted a brace.

"What usually happens?"

"I put it in and get them to count to twenty to show them that they can. The next time I see them they have accommodated to it"

"Can they sing with it in?"

"I've never asked. I can't remember fitting an appliance to anyone who said they sang"

I was to remember that without recognising its significance.

On the way back to the school I had to stop for petrol and as I stood with the hose directed into the tank I realised I would have to converse with the lady in the service station and other people I did not know.

"Why are you doing this? You have no problem with teeth. Take the thing out. You have had it in for two hours and that is enough."

As I replaced the hose in the pump I wanted to flee – not have to face the cashier. I walked to the window and spoke without looking at her. To look at her would have destroyed my control. I felt I couldn't speak, yet tried hard to speak and what came out was just a wee bit drunk, not enough to prompt a call for the traffic police but yet enough to force a patronising smile. As I drove away I frantically sucked the brace and that made me feel better. It occurred to me that I may have stepped over the divide into pathology; innocently placed myself in special needs.

Three weeks on and I was still sucking the brace and all its bits of wire. In classes I ran my tongue around the wire on my front teeth and there seemed no relief from this constant sucking except when I took it out to sing. I knew that when I suspended the whole body to sing the tongue moved to the back of my mouth and didn't touch my front teeth at all. I decided to try singing with it in to beat this habit of the tongue constantly coming forward and sucking the brace.

After a few days my speech became much clearer, but even more surprising things happened. At the end of my daily practice; after rolling and singing, hanging and singing, I routinely stood upright and still to sing a song. The voice, which had improved with the body stretch and movement, had always previously returned to its normal husk and strain the moment I did this, but I persevered just in case today was the day when my voice just might… When I sang with the brace in and stretched my tongue away from it as I yelped my vowels I thought my tongue would tear from the floor of my mouth. When I stood up after this my neck and shoulders felt free and the sound was definitely better.

Dentists appear more than any other profession in the nightmares of the common man and so they generally do not talk about what they do except to each other. Once I had this 'thing 'in my mouth I began to meet dentists. It was like rolling up my trouser leg. I immediately began to get the handshake. At concerts, the folk club, the pub, I frequently attracted the attention of a dentist although I could never before remember anyone ever admitting publicly to being one. I concluded that it must be very unusual for someone in their fifties to have metal in her mouth. Eventually I met a dentist at a house warming party who was more than usually curious about my motives.

"I had to discover what your dentist was doing as it appears to be entirely the wrong appliance for the dental problem you have. I would hesitate to put that particular device in at all because it crosses the roof of the mouth and if you wear it for too long you will jam your cranium".

"Pardon?"

"The bones of your head have to move. Those devices which bridge the two halves of the palate have been abandoned by some of us. There is a danger it will jam the cranial rhythm. Are you aware that the bones of your head need the freedom to move? "

"I'm just learning about it on my course"

Had he mentioned this just six months before he would have lost me but I was learning to feel the cranial rhythm in classes at the school. Someone lay face up on a table, you cradled their head between your two hands and waited to feel the rhythm of a movement. I had never yet felt any movement at all in anyone's head and no one else had yet felt it in mine but I comforted myself with the thought that it must be stronger in some people than in others. However no one had ever mentioned the possibility of 'jamming' it.

Here was a medically main stream dentist discussing things I was learning on a course that came under the umbrella of 'Alternative Therapy'. He was also behaving somewhat unprofessionally by questioning what the orthodontist was doing for me. She had already told me that you had to be licensed by General Dental Council (GDC) as an orthodontist before you could move teeth about. All kinds of whistles and sirens were starting up in my head and I needed to hang on to this conversation.

"There are all kinds of questions I would like to ask" he went on, "for instance…"

I filled two plates with food and we found a small greenhouse at the back of the house lined with green tomatoes. Two upturned buckets served as seats and he opened with…

"..do you find that cross-bite you have effects the way that you sing?"

All the little tomatoes on all their little stalks shook all their little bells. It was deafening.

"Something affects the way that I sing. Something affects everything about me, everything I do or want to do. I have ability, commitment and I need to love and be loved. Yet I fail. There appears to be no answer to it, at least so far. What is a cross-bite?"

"The upper and lower teeth fit together into a 'bite' and when this bite is correct it completes the balancing of the whole skeleton, which is your frame. This ability to balance on two feet gives strength to the whole body, The technical term for the meeting of the teeth is 'occlusion' and a cross bite is a particular incorrect meeting of the teeth, called a malocclusion... I'm sorry, I shouldn't be telling you all this, it can be upsetting for someone to be on the receiving end of this kind of observation. I don't really know you. "

He picked up his empty plate and prepared to go but I was already planning the moving of my teeth into a reasonable, what was that word, occlusion? I already knew from the singing orthodontist that it could be done.

"There is nothing you can say to me that will hurt more than I hurt already. Thirty years ago I thought I was losing my voice but now I know I was losing my life and no one recognised it. I have to halt this accelerating downward spiral because everything is getting worse. If there is any information I can use I want it. I want to learn how to sing again because I know I can then go home, wherever home might be".

He looked hard at me for a few moments and then produced a torch and peered into my mouth.

"Your jaw has slid to the left for some reason and the back teeth only meet at the tooth edge. On the right side, for instance, the lower outside tooth edge meets the upper inside tooth edge. This creates all kinds of problems. You may grind your teeth, they look worn down. Two spaces have been bridged but you still have too many gaps so you lack skeletal support. Your lower front teeth have leaned to the left and moved out of any kind of arch, there's got to be a reason for that. That is what is going on in the teeth. It is much more important to know what is happening to the balance and position of the jaw at the joint that the jaw makes with the skull – the TMJ".

"TMJ?"

"The Temporo Mandibular Joint"

He sounded it out slowly as one would teach a child the language it needs to live a life. Why had I never heard a term so relevant to my education? He produced a small hand mirror out of his pocket and told me to put my forefingers in my ears with my hands facing forward. If I then pressed on the front of the ear hole I located the joint between the jaw and the skull. Looking in the mirror I opened my mouth slowly as wide as I could and then closed it again. I did this several times before I could believe that the same travel would repeat itself.

As my mouth opened the jaw skewed to the left until it executed a little chicane before reaching the limit. On the way back it came to a halt, there was a sharp crack under my right finger and a chicane in the other direction before my mouth finally closed.

"You have a locked out disc. Between the knob at the skull end of your jaw, called the condyle, and the curve it fits into under the skull there is a cushioning device, a disc which slides forward when your mouth opens. When the jaw is skewed, one condyle moves further into the joint than the other and compacts the disc on that side, and over time the disc gets locked out of the joint. The crack is the disc stretched to the limit by this lock out and then snapping back into the joint. Have you ever had any jaw pain?

"I had lots of toothache in my early twenties, but teeth were extracted and it went away".

"You have been very lucky. You could have had all kinds of symptomatic pain from that bite".

I had to pause a moment to control my breathing,

"I *have* had all kinds of symptomatic pain from this bite. I seem to have a very low response to physical pain. I just don't seem to feel it any more. Pain for me now is what I seem to do to everyone close to me. When I should be responding sympathetically to those I love I drive them away with my manic energy and the hardness of my voice. Sometimes when I speak I can't believe what I hear. People are supposed to get weaker as they get older aren't they? Well I get stronger; drive myself in a manic perpetual motion. Behind this façade I am so emotionally weak that I let people bully me, seduce me, tell me lies and I am totally unable to fight back. You remember the lion in The Wizard of Oz? Well that's me. All roar and nothing else. " Tears were coming thick and fast. They soaked my shirt and his handkerchief, which he had given me when they began.

I blew my nose, felt better for that and smiled.

"That's not quite right. I haven't got a roar. The whole purpose of all this is to get my roar back. You know about teeth, I'm learning about voices. If we put it all together maybe I can find some answers for people like me"

"We'll go to my clinic. I have diagrams that will explain things. There may be some answers for you. I've never thought about the voice bit. I don't meet people who sing, at least they don't tell me they do."

"The orthodontist said that. It's strange. They're so close, the voice and the teeth. You'd think they would fall over one another. I want you to fix my teeth and I may find a connection".

At 3am in his surgery I had my first real functional anatomy lesson and although everything was a revelation to me, I knew that it all made sense.

"Uprightness is maintained by the law of equal and opposite and you have a set of reflexly operated postural muscles to maintain your upright balance. If your jaw is over to one side muscles on the other side of your neck have to be added to the reflex muscle system pull that heavy head as upright as possible. You teeth come together roughly 2,000 times a day when you swallow. That gives you a balance reference and stabilizes the structure-the skeleton. When *your* teeth come together emergency lights flash in your head because of the cross bite and muscles will tense all over your body to prevent your falling over. Everything must be a great effort; moving about, walking, sitting, lifting, because the muscles needed for those things were already working overtime helping out with keeping you on your feet "

He kept looking at me nervously as if he expected me to react to all this in some adverse way but I drank in his words as though it were some wondrous elixir; water after a gruelling journey through white hot sand. Everything he said opened another clenched and painful fist in my brain, sometimes those I had plunged deep into my pain with the hopelessness of ever dealing with it.

"Your autonomic system will try very hard to put your teeth together in a better bite. For instance, you may grind your teeth at night or bite your nails."

"What about twisting your face so that you can bite the inside of your cheek?"

"If you examine which side you bite you will probably find that you twist and chew the cheek the opposite way to the jaw swing. You are making a vain effort to pull your jaw straight"

"I bit my nails all my life and I began to chew my cheek when I was about eleven. I remember doing it in exams to help me think. I'm still doing it. Can I possibly have had this cross-bite all my life?"

I told him about the removal of my wisdom teeth, expecting him to confirm what I had already worked out, that the operation had been the cause of my crooked jaw and my crashed voice.

"The operation was significant but probably not the cause. It was more likely the last straw that finally tipped you over the edge. Your problems seem to have begun in your late teens"

I remembered the sixth form work that I just couldn't cope with. The essays I couldn't write, the extra tuition I ducked.

"We do have a Physiological Adaptive Range, (PAR). It's like money in the bank. When something traumatic happens to us and the organism cannot cope, we use up some of this PAR. But it is draining your capitol. You are draining away the body's physical bank account and it is not a bottomless pit. We have to put money back into the bank. Exercise and understanding allow you to recover natural voice, body and brain patterns if you keep learning and questioning established practice. This restores Adaptive Range to within its limits. If you just go on draining the capitol it usually runs out in about fifteen years. That would take us back to your birth. Do you know anything about your birth? Was it natural and easy, or were there problems in your delivery? For instance, were forceps used?"

It seemed bizarre that there could be a connection between my birth and the way my teeth came together. I was born without teeth and these teeth were the second lot, not the first. However, there *was* a difficult birth and I told him about it.

"That is where your problems began. Many babies experience slight birth trauma, nothing that you can see in the appearance of the baby but the voice can be a great indicator of distress. The baby may cry a lot for no apparent reason, or be totally the opposite, much too quiet. "

I could remember my mother saying what a beautiful, calm and well behaved baby I was "You never cried once". As if to make up for that I began to cry again now, sobbing uncontrollably.

"Why didn't somebody see? Why didn't somebody do something – the doctor, the midwife. My mother probably didn't know but why didn't they…?"

He let me cry for a while. This was not a dentist as I recognised one.

"You can't blame anyone. That was fifty years ago. No one knew what to look for. Now it is different. A baby can be checked by a cranial osteopath or a cranial chiropractor within a few days of being born. Don't look backwards but forward to putting it right. I have no idea how correcting your jaw will affect your voice, but your balance and the stress you experience in your life can improve. However I can't guarantee anything, and you are the oldest person I have met that has shown an interest in this kind of correction but you can certainly be saved from becoming any worse. If your teeth and jaw are left like that the stress on your whole life can only increase and there is considerable evidence to suggest that this can lead to chronic illness."

But I was not listening any more to what would happen to me, my mind was elsewhere.

"What about my children? They were born about twenty five years ago. When they were born no one suggested that they should be checked and they were both difficult births. According to what you have told me, my whole life has been dominated by the problems I developed when I was born. What about them? Where was the information for my babies?"

The tears were starting again. I could see a pattern of damage going from generation to generation through the mothers and the birth process. My daughter would have children and that may continue the structural damage she inherited at her own birth. What had my mother done to me and what had I passed on to my daughter and her children? My mind was in chaos. The whole progression took on nightmare proportions and I could see the babies she produced with severe motor and brain defects...But he saw the panic he had caused, took both of my hands in his and calmly explained the bigger picture. I listened very carefully because this now did not only affect me and my life but the lives of everyone I cared about.

He told me he had trained as a dentist, passed all his exams and been licensed to practice by the General Dental Council. He had intended to pursue the post graduate course in Orthodontics but his wife was pregnant and he needed the money from the practice to set up home and have her stop work. He wanted to continue to learn so he went on all the dental courses that he could.

"These courses taught me how to refine and perfect what I already knew".

One day a leaflet appeared in the practice advertising courses in dentistry that looked 'beyond the teeth'. These leaflets, which were from America and Australia, suggested that to make decisions about the teeth without considering their effect on the whole body could cause health problems not previously associated with the teeth and jaw. The feedback from the teeth to the brain was so direct that if someone had malocclusion (like me) over a number of years it would change their whole posture down to their feet. These courses were encouraging dentists to work with, and listen to, other disciplines that worked with the head and neck and whole body posture, like cranial osteopaths, for instance.

He went to America with the money saved to train as an orthodontist and was introduced to the concept of interdisciplinary treatment, which meant that in order to correct someone's malocclusion he had to work with someone who could explain to him why these teeth had moved into this position in the first place. If you corrected them without treating the rest of the body, the teeth were likely to move back after treatment, or the jaw return to its painful position.

"It was suggested on the course that I needed to work with disciplines that could supply information on early development and posture, neither of which were even mentioned in my training as a dentist. It was also suggested that the summary extraction of teeth for crowding was unnecessary in most cases. The bone structure could be expanded to fit the teeth. This caused me to work in quite a different way, looking at the whole patient and not just the teeth. I had to step out of the NHS because their guidelines for treatment are very limiting. To expand the bone structure of the jaw to fit the teeth I need to fit appliances, but my licensing board does not consider me sufficiently trained. At this stage I am supposed to refer my patient to a registered orthodontist.

I will need a very well worded consent form from you if you wish me to correct your jaw or I may be struck off the dental register for unprofessional practice. You need to realise that if you are to work with me to discover the better function of your jaw, your balance, posture and the recovery of your voice you will be working with someone who belongs to a growing number of dentists who are considered to be rebels within their own profession".

"From my personal experience I know an orthodontist. We have been working together to discover how braces affect the way children speak. I could go to her..."

"She may well not know what you are talking about. This treatment is called 'Functional Orthopaedics' It involves moving bones as well as teeth and expanding the dental arches instead of continually extracting teeth. The mainstream British Dental Establishment has some way to go before taking this leap. Once you do take this leap you realise that the fundamental training of dentists, always a poor relation in the medical field, is now way out of date. Not only can we move the bones of the face and expand dental arches to prevent tooth crowding, we can also begin to sort out those problems early in children's lives, so that by the time they are teenagers experiencing real difficulties with hormonal changes and discovering how to grow up, their teeth and jaws are helping them to cope with all this. They are confident and attractive, with good posture. We can begin correcting children's *future* dental problems by doing *preventative* treatment, which is all over by thirteen years old. It is also much more cost effective".

I had stopped sliding into oblivion. I had reasons for my nail biting, my cheek chewing. I did not understand many of the connections he made between my problems and my teeth, but this was definitely the best information I had ever had and I just needed to study it and spend time on the details. Someone actually seemed to understand what was wrong with me. Most of all, a diagnosis and maintenance system seemed to be developing that would also help my children and grandchildren. I was absolutely fascinated by the concept of all parts of me being connected. When I was biting my nails, was I chewing away at my voice?

A conservative estimate of time to correct a dental and postural problem so embedded in my life on someone as old as me would be about five years, that is if it were possible to correct. There was no guarantee. During that time I would need several different appliances which would no doubt make talking and possibly singing pretty difficult. Changes in my jaw and teeth would affect my head and neck muscles, many of which were in permanent spasm to accommodate for the bite problem. Could I get them working again or had my brain been out of touch with them for so long that they were dead to me?

I needed help to encourage the muscles I was using to hold myself up to relax and create a domino effect that would travel through my posture and change how I stood on the floor. It explained so much of the balance problems. I would need treatment from a cranial osteopath or cranial chiropractor *'who understood the dental connection'.* This phrase would haunt me in my dealings with singing for the rest of my life. I needed to work with clinicians who were prepared to work together and discuss my progress because I wanted to understand what was going to happen to me. I also needed to take part in my recovery, be empowered by it as I had been disempowered by what had happened to me so far. The plan to help me that I had discovered was light years beyond any treatment or education I had ever had before.

My voice teachers had been totally disinterested in my wisdom extractions or my balance problems, the surgeon who carried out the wisdom extractions never knew I could sing because he was not interested in anything but the job he had to do in my mouth and anyway I always felt powerless in the face of medical authority. In all the years of struggle, all the terrible pain of knowing I was unable to cope no one had been prepared to look beyond the problem that was presented. I was isolated and disempowered but no one wanted to know how I felt and I was afraid to express what I felt was wrong in case it brought in yet another consultant to deal with yet another, differently perceived problem.

I had finally described my pain and cried over it for the first time in front of this dentist because he had struck some chord within me. I was passionate about finding my voice, always had been and this man displayed as much passion for the new way he had begun to work. I cried to him with the relief of finding another person with a passion for something he believed in and working against considerable odds. He was also the first medical person to look at all of me – not just my voice, not just my physical problems or the stress I was demonstrating. I would never have dared collapse before any of the medical people who had previously dealt with me. I knew that any such display would be seen as evidence that I needed counselling, or a drug to calm me down, or maybe pep me up.

So what was the next move? I never doubted for one moment that I wanted to go this route but how to manage it? I would be fifty nine before the work was completed, and that was only if there were no interferences on the way. But I couldn't afford to dwell too long on either my age or things that may happen to me in the next five years. Life was not a dress rehearsal. 'What if?'....had no place in this decision.

I needed a secure and supportive base for those five years and more importantly, it needed to be within reach of a dentist skilful in these techniques. There were precious few of those scattered about the country and I must link up with one like Joe, who was prepared to work *with* me as well as treat me, explain everything and be the sounding board for all I could discover about the voice. I also had to work with a structural clinician who would no doubt find problems in my body related to those of my teeth. My body may change as my teeth and jaw became a more integral part of good posture and I knew from experience that any change can be painful and traumatic. Change for the good was still change. I intended to earn my living by teaching singing, which for me required lots of physical exercise so the whole programme may be even more difficult to cope with that anyone could imagine.

This work was only available from private dental practice and the cost of correction may well run into thousands. Even though Joe understood my commitment he wanted me to be sure.

"You must remember that leaving everything alone is not life threatening. Many people with far worse dental problems than yours live happy and satisfying lives. They never notice the problem and have no pain. Don't ask me why. It is one of life's great mysteries. If you can solve that, dentists who practice functional orthopaedics will be very grateful. Even if you do have all this corrected there is no guarantee that your problems will go away. It may not affect your singing. However, if you do decide to go ahead dig out photographs of yourself from infancy and arrange them chronologically. You may be able to see these problems developing. It will also help the dentist to plan the treatment."

I knew the decision had been made in the greenhouse. It was made *for* me and not *by* me. I blamed the tomatoes. I drove away and sat in the early sun in a cornfield to decide what came next. I had already taken the experimental appliance out of my mouth and now I threw it as far as I could. It had served its purpose. I had one year left of my course and money was rapidly running out. I had to do some serious teaching soon and make financial plans.

I lay back, looked up at the sky and recalled the fall down the steps where I felt nothing of pain. How far could this accommodation system really go? Could it make you so strong, so capable that you felt nothing? Could you shut out pain altogether? Shut out emotion? Could you do things to people you loved and not see their hurt because you were limited by the insensitivity you had developed to protect you from pain? Supposing when I fell I had just arrived at the point when I could no longer hold myself together, all ability to compensate finally exhausted. Is that why I collapsed in the bathroom? There was a limit, within one mind and body, to how far you can push. What did he call it? Physiological Adaptive Range. And what happened then? I sang out of tune and that began my search for a reason why. The search led me to roll on the floor in the church and discover climbing and suspending my body. Hanging from something would straighten me up, that's why I sang better. When I stood up I went back to leaning and preventing myself falling over. That affected my singing. Why didn't my singing teachers know that? I never knew how weak I really was. And then did a larger and stronger animal devour you?

When my Aunt died I was financially secure, with a job, a house, the children content in their schools and their lives. What would have happened if I had stayed alone and taken responsibility for bringing my children up alone and making a life for all of us? Did I know deep down that I was not strong enough to do that? Did I let him relieve me of all responsibility because I knew I was heading for some terrible breakdown if he didn't? Evolution drives survival. Did the wounded lioness with cubs seize her chance to survive and refuse to see it as anything but love?

I remembered the ledger that organised my housekeeping, set out by him so that even birthday presents had a budget and extra petrol had to be justified. When I earned cash for my teaching he collected it from me and banked it himself, "for convenience". I joked about his signing 'paid in by…' Then I changed, began to fight back. Why and when did I do that?

There was the trip to the bank to demand a cheque book. Why had I been so surprised that I should do that? It now seemed a right and proper thing for me to have access to our money and knowledge of its movement. Why had I needed that cheque? I wanted the bridges from the dentist. It was when I had the bridges fitted that I first began to question his actions and my dependence. What did Joe say about strength?

"The more teeth that meet the stronger and more balanced you are..."

And what about that shift of my tongue? It was still there now, resting against the back of my palate and those teeth that were fitted as bridges. Did I suddenly find a better balance in myself after that? I got up and stretched my arms up to the blue sky. I was not going back to that powerless woman, ever.

"I will go home and tackle the question of a divorce settlement. Half of the value of the house is mine. I will use it to buy myself a house where I can teach and earn. The rest will pay for this correction so that I can S- I- I-I –NG! A-A-A-A-A-H-H-H! I shouted to the sky and then sang a song I had struggled with for twenty years. I sang it at full throttle with my horrible voice ringing out over the field. I didn't care. It was all going to be different.

At my next tutorial I launched into what I had learned with great enthusiasm. As I saw it I had two terms left and if, as the dentist said, my neck and shoulder tension were caused by my 'bite', correction may solve the problem of why my head would absolutely not go forward and up. I may be able to balance on two feet and sit in comfort at meditation. Would my behaviour change? Would I be calmer in the face of frustration? Certainly I wanted to discuss the jaw information and also question why none of this information had appeared as part of my course. F M Alexander's work was about balance and posture and certainly posture was apparently affected by the teeth and jaw. He had begun his research into posture by having voice problems, so he knew that voice and posture were connected. This information on jaws and teeth and how they affect posture may open up a whole new area of research for those studying the technique.

"You are here to study Alexander's writings and the principles of The Technique. If you were directing your body with sufficient commitment to those principles you could correct all those problems yourself. Direction makes all changes possible. You are seeking avoidance and hunting for distractions. You have only two terms left to qualify and you need every bit of that time working 'hands on' at the school if I am to be satisfied that you understand the principles with both mind and body. You need to give up all teaching for the rest of the course and concentrate on yourself and this work. I will give you extra tuition and when you have qualified you can pursue other lines of enquiry. But not while you are on this course."

You cannot not know what you know. Both my mind and my body already had this information. I had already begun to watch people, look at their teeth and jaw and now I could only see that behind the Director's beard he hardly opened his mouth to speak and his face muscles appeared 'set' in a fixed expression. His voice was always very pale and monotonous. We had had several 'spats' about his refusal to attempt to sing. All I could think of was getting his beard off and looking at the position of his jaw – and I hadn't even started work on my own teeth yet. How could I possibly ever be taught by him again and button up my curiosity.

I did try, but at the same time I requested that my dentist friend be invited to give the school a presentation on the new dentistry from America and Australia. The connection between Alexander Technique and dental misalignment was not accepted and the request refused. I could not understand how any professional body would refuse to even *hear* information that might be relevant and move its knowledge base forward.

After an evening with a physiotherapist also interested in how my teeth and jaw had developed, the struggle to qualify as an Alexander Teacher became irrelevant. I had spent nearly three years attempting to think my way into the following improvements

- Let the neck be free to allow the head to roll forward and up in such a way that the back can lengthen and widen.
- Widen across the upper part of the arms
- Let the knees go forward and away

I now knew that the aids to my recovery were more numerous and more varied than the principles by which I was supposed to qualify and I could no longer curb my curiosity.

I talked about my new findings with other students, at lunch, in the pub and in breaks between classes. Just before the end of my last term I was asked to leave the school unqualified, because I was a disruptive influence.

It seemed at first to be just one more illustration of the behaviour that had driven my life so far. I had been disruptive in so many different contexts. After each occasion I would suffer an aftermath of self recrimination when I would rush around feeling desperate and trying to put right what I had done and make people love me again.

This time there was none of that. I hadn't yet begun the dental correction or any of the work to correct my balance or posture but I knew that I had finally found people to work with that were asking elsewhere the questions not being answered in their own field of expertise. They were all willing to work together across different disciplines to find answers. I had already met a cranial chiropractor, a dentist, and a physiotherapist, all of whom were willing to test their own skill in open discussion to find an answer to my problems. None of them considered me mad, badly behaved or unable to cope. They were all interested in what had happened to my voice and whether that was the result of the problems they could individually see. That was all I had ever wanted. I couldn't believe that at last I had actually found help.

I like the things which snatch the wind
In Sailfuls, wheelfuls, handfuls.
Squeeze it into pockets, pistons, spinnakers,
Pressurize it tight and when it's bursting -
Hurl it out behind, then roaring on, grab more.
I like to straddle the cushion of excitement,
While eyes and skin are whipped by spray and steam.
Stream along in pouring rain, and screaming wind,
Coat billowing behind.
I yearn for tracks and treads and trails
And undertow my spirit has not played with.
When all these wonders fail to take away my breath -
Then take away my breath.

Chapter 13: The Nails

Mother's grave in North Wales had been unmarked for five years because for a long time I could not decide what to put on the headstone. She had bought a double grave on the death of her first husband, expecting to be buried beside him. Then life changed and she had a second husband. When he died she buried him beside the first and in later years, first accepting and later quite enjoying her second widowhood, she joked that she would one day lie between them.

It was the day after mother died and the little Welshman all reverently in black called to see me at her house. In a small community one knows even the funeral director.

"Oh, I'm so upset. What will she think of me? She always said "Bury me between them and I'll be happy" and you see – there's no room. She paid for everything ages ago, even the headstone, but there's no room for her you see. It's a double grave, not meant for three. I didn't know that, she never said. I've just checked for Friday, opening it up. There's nowhere to open up. I don't know what to do. There isn't another place vacant in the old cemetery. She's had that one since 1930."

I took him in like a sad stray and gave him the obligatory funereal sherry. We sat and thought about it and the more we thought about it the funnier it seemed. She would have enjoyed the dilemma, the idea of this poor little man having nowhere to put her. After two sherries the solution became clear to me.

"She would fit if she were cremated. We could sprinkle the ashes between her two husbands and her wish would be granted. "

"Oh I don't know if she'd like that. She never mentioned anything about cremation…."

"Let's put it this way. She bought the grave in the first place at a time when money was very tight for her. Goodness knows how she afforded a double grave in the main cemetery. If anyone deserves to be there, she does"

So it was decided, the burial complete and now five years later, all problems solved I was to go and see the grave with my mother between her two husbands and the headstone engraved and in place. I also had to make my peace with her.

I sat on the grass beside the grave and looked down at my recovered hands. Since the coming of the dentist I had stopped biting my nails and even cheek chewing. Knowing why I was doing it gave me a measure of control. I had to explain all this to my mother.

"It was my teeth. I was trying to get my jaw to be comfortable. My jaw muscles were going into spasm because my teeth did not fit together. Dentists took out more and more teeth but everything still hurt. When I had bitten my nails down to the quick that's when the cheek chewing took over, I'm sorry about that too but I do want you to see that it really wasn't my fault. Look at my hands now. My nails are painted.

I'm sorry I wasn't there when you died. I had to drive from Suffolk when the hospital phoned and when I arrived you were already laid in the Chapel. I wanted to take your hand but as I leaned down I saw the manicured nails, beautifully shaped and painted silver. I had come straight to you from gardening and my nails were black from shelling broad beans. I put my hands in my apron pockets when I leaned to kiss you so you could not see the stubby fingers, the bitten black nails. The nurse returned to see me saying goodbye to my mother with my hands nonchalantly in my pockets.

I have recently grown my nails into these amazing talons, just for you. They don't really go with my life but I'm happy to do it just once so that we will both know that I can. Now watch very carefully mother. I am going to take these scissors and cut them off. Do you see? I am cutting them to the length that allows me to play the piano and to do lots of other things that I find really irksome and frustrating with these great nails. This is my choice and my nails are not ugly any more even at this sensible and functional length.

Since you died something else has happened to my hands. I broke some fingers, so I'll never have hands quite like yours however much I try. I'm so glad that it happened after you died because it would have been even worse for you than the nail biting. The joints look a bit swollen but my hands are OK now and I can play the piano just the same. All of my fingers are functional and that is the most important thing to me. You will have to try and forgive me this attitude.

If you were here now I would be able to tell you about the broken fingers without losing control. I always felt I had to defend everything because I had this sense of my own incompetence. I am still unbalanced and my behaviour is still erratic but I have help now and I know that balance and behaviour are going to change, so I no longer believe I am going mad. I shall sit here beside you and tell you about the hands calmly and in a way that may even make you proud of me. It would have choked me with failure before I felt I had people on my side and I knew how important it was for you that I was a success. Maybe that is why I was always so on the attack.

I was teaching in London to earn enough money to keep me and the children so that he could run his business without financial constraints. Everything about this was wrong. I could have stopped him leaving his family for me but instead I helped him to do it, in spite of knowing how much pain I would inflict on so many people, especially the children. It meant that I left my own children for two days each week, having just uprooted them from their father, school and friends. There mother, you never thought to hear me say that I was wrong, stupid, wicked even. Maybe we never really got past the nail biting. I knew *that* was wrong and stupid but I could not help it. I could not stop that little thing any more than I could stop this world shattering one. Unable to control my decisions I could only defend them.

"I will not be your mistress!" Meanwhile I made all the necessary arrangements to be it. I argued about leaving my children to work in London meanwhile booking students for weeks ahead in my London Studio. I argued that he should be able to provide for us while I made arrangements to make my personal account a joint one in case .....in case of what? In case I was not loved otherwise. I protested my desire to be a wife and mother; that I wanted nothing more than to be at home and cook and garden and *be* there for my family, but I went to London to teach.

How could I be so stupid? We were not a family. He had a mistress who happened to have two children. How could I lose all those important values out of my life? How? When I argued, protested, tried to have a voice in this affair he would listen attentively, nod wisely, agree with me and then sidestep. My throat would tighten, my head panic and I'd completely lose track of what I wanted to say.

So I got up at 5am on Wednesday mornings having kissed my children goodnight and goodbye on Tuesday night. By 8.30am Wednesday I was teaching singing in a studio in London and on the Thursday I moved myself to the other end of the city to take classes all day in a converted school. By supper on Thursday I was back home having brought in enough money to keep my part of the family for the week.

Could you believe that the daughter you trained to be a caring mother, supportive friend, respecter of persons: a daughter who read to her children and taught them music could be so crassly and insensitively stupid? That the little girl who played the piano and sang, was financially independent… ? Sorry, I need a break to calm down".

I walked down the cemetery and laid my forehead against a tree. Stretch your arms out sideways and feel the stretch of your fingers against the cool rough bark. Unwind the coiled spring. That's better. No going back into shifting the blame, whining about not being able to help it. I could take responsibility for myself now. I had been about to launch into… "If I had had treatment when I was born, if a cranial osteopath had checked me at about a week old, things may have been different"

"One day I will have to tell you that I had to struggle through the birth canal of a woman with a misaligned pelvis. But I will have to tell you without you shouldering all the mess of my life because you could not know. You did your absolute best for me. I have to tell you when the time is right and I have learned more about it. It will come when we are closer again as we were when I was little. Now I am telling you about my broken fingers".

I went back to sit on the grass

"Leaving the children was terrible. I woke on every Wednesday morning praying that something would happen to prevent my going. Why did I just not go? Over time I developed a way of not caring, not about them, but about me. I channelled my whole mind and body to achieving maximum financial return and convinced myself that I was providing for them. I taught right through the day from 8.30 am to 9pm without a stop so that I could not think of them.

Deep down I knew this was a recipe for disaster. I drove to London with a warning flashing in my head telling me that there was no one to protect my children if I wrapped myself around a tree, but I convinced myself that I absolutely *had* to bring the money home. My lover dictated that it was my responsibility. I was in this place with my children because it was what I had said I wanted. I could not dispute that, yet my mind constantly warred with itself, now putting my children first, then being seduced by flattery.

On this particular morning I arrived in my teaching room to find the upright piano facing the wall, the keyboard against the wall and inaccessible. My head was not actually in this place. It was watching my children prepare for school. Would they remember to take their dinner money? Would they bring that stupid boy home, like last Thursday. He was obviously a boy who has no settled home, anyone could tell. But if I am here, working away for two days, have *my* children a settled home? It was a different world mother and I was not coping with it.

With these thoughts tumbling in my head and also planning my day I strode purposefully across the room and pulled the piano away from the wall to turn it round. The top of it came ever so slowly towards me while the bottom stayed against the wall where the castors were lodged against the planking on the floor. Terrified of the whole thing breaking through the floor and dropping into the restaurant below I tried desperately to slow it down, but in the last seconds had to leap out of the way. That was when I first discovered that there was no co-ordination between my left and right sides. The left hand leaped out of the way, the right went down under the piano, not quick enough to avoid the sharp brass hinge on the lid, which tore into the flesh of my palm and dragged my open hand and me down with the toppling piano till I landed on my knees alongside its crash, speechless, mindless with pain from the hand still trapped underneath. When the disaster struck all I could think of was how I would ever get home to my children.

"My dear try to free your neck. Someone get her some arnica"- (the homeopathic remedy for shock).

None of this dealt with the piano which pinned me to the floor. The piano facing the wall was in a School for the Study of the Alexander Technique in London and I gave singing classes as part of the course. The director wanted the students to experience singing to each other because when questioned they had listed it as one of the fundamental terrors (How long has singing been like this?) I was hired to introduce this fear in the face of which they must free the neck.

I did not move. The only stirring in my dead head was a little grey mouse which lifted its tiny nose, twitched its whiskers and said

"Now how will you ever play the piano again?"

The mouse's nose was very pink. Then it turned red. Then the mouse turned red and lost its shape and stopped being a mouse. It became a red spreading blot that leapt out of my head and onto the floor under the piano. It was creeping out now where the piano was attached to my wrist.

The irrelevant voice went away, possibly to find the arnica, and was replaced by one I recognised as the French student who was paying her way through the course by cooking the lunches.

In my classes she could not bring herself to sing for the group. I encouraged, cajoled and even bullied her, then backtracked and comforted. She had finally sung in the class the week before, standing alone in the middle of the room. She sang in French and I put my arms around her from behind to halt the fluttering in her diaphragm. After finishing her song she burst into tears and declared it was the hardest thing she had ever done.

"The stillness, the open-ness, the vulnerability was so difficult. I felt undressed before the world. I was describing how I really was; how I was on the inside. My failings, my soft bits, all were on show. However could I ever protect myself again? Everyone that heard me sing today would know all of me. It made me cry for myself, for my safety".

She must have recruited people to lift the piano because my hand was back with me, wrapped in a teacloth that said, "Tourist London". Buckingham Palace was on top while Big Ben held my shattered fingers together and Green Park turned red.

I gave myself to her as the lion to Androcles and she took over my life. She ordered a taxi to take me to casualty at St Bartholemew's Hospital. She held me like a speechless baby on the journey and then strode through a crowded reception area and placed me down in the only empty cubicle, reverting to French when unable to get her own way. She found a young doctor and demanded his attention for me, holding his sleeve so that he could not escape. He was Australian and looked about nine years old.

"I am a pianist. I have to play. I can't lose my music" I held up my visitor's London and he took it away. The first three fingers had been bent back and broken between first and second joint, the flesh left gaping by the brass hinge on the piano lid.

The mouse was back. Soft brown eyes filled with tears. "Poor little fingers, caught in a trap. Snap goes the spring and no more music". The nine year old doctor sat beside me.

"There are two ways to deal with this. The first is that I take total responsibility. I will give you a general anaesthetic and straighten your fingers, stitch you up and support the damage with strapping. You will be unconscious for several hours and have to stay overnight in hospital. You will be pain free but you will never play again because even by the time you regain consciousness excess scar tissue will have formed. You will lose touch with yourself at a vital time when you need to be in charge of yourself.

If I straighten your fingers and stitch you up without any anaesthetic you can walk out of here, go find a piano and begin to teach your fingers to play again. The second way is a joint responsibility between me and you. It will be pain all the way but you will not lose touch with yourself and you will play again if you work at it. It rather depends on how much pain you can stand. I am very busy. You have five minutes to decide"

He was gone. I sat there wondering how someone could become so wise in such a short life. Then I attempted to make the reasonable decision but even the mouse refused to support it. The mouse was followed closely by you, mother. You took me on the back of your bike every Thursday to my lessons and sat in the cold while I played. Then there was the angel who had guided and supported me throughout my practice until I could really play; the angel who changed and became my devil within. The devil within who will be tamed, may even revert to an angel when I am balanced upright on two feet and free of all these tense muscles.

The day was very peaceful, the grass around the grave very soft and green. The story I was telling had gone from my head and I was aware only of the stillness in the cemetery. I felt I'd missed something. What had I just been talking about? I had wanted to thank my mother for giving me my music and my angel for encouraging it. In the stillness the smell of the warm grass made it all clear. My mother was the angel. She had given me my music. She nurtured it and gave me the kind of childhood that encouraged it to develop into part of my life. She and dad together gave me a value system that kept me practicing when it was hard, until I loved music and singing so much that when I lost it I had to find the reason and get it back. She read me poetry and made it important in my life, although she left school when she was twelve. She was my angel, there wasn't an imaginary presence that came floating down to praise my musical efforts, the praise was in the uphill cycling with a large child on the back of the bike.

And the devil? Maybe she had been devil too, because she bore me and she caused the birth trauma that had never been corrected and that had ruined my life so far. But she had also passed on to me the courage that had kept her going after her first husband's death, her ability to work physically hard and not give up and that would finally enable me to correct the birth trauma that she could not possibly know about and start again at fifty five. This was also her gift. If my father was the joy in my life, my mother was the strength. A great weight was lifted as if I had been struggling to know my mother all of my life and now I did. I could finish my story.

"OK, What's it to be?

For the first time I noticed that the doctor was Australian and when I agreed to plan two he immediately gained twenty years. I knew I must have made the right decision because the world suddenly contained everything that I needed. I stretched my left hand out into space in panic to find another grasping it. The nurse who did that also held me down and shushed me as I cried and clutched at the mouse in my head, trying to crush it, kill it, transfer what I could not bear into some being used to pain and torment. The mouse in my head just seemed to fit the bill. The mature experienced doctor I was lucky to find got on with the job in spite of me.

"I've changed my mind. Don't touch me. I want to duck out, avoid this too much pain. GET HIM OFF ME!"

I might as well have been a noisy lawnmower whirring away in the background. He stitched up the gashes in my hand, straightened my fingers one by hellish one and applied a loose bandage.

"Move them! This one... THIS ONE!"

One by one we tried them out together, me, the nurse, the mouse and the grown up doctor.

"OK, that's it. Off you go and find a piano"

Back at the school everyone was still in shock. When I walked in and resumed my timetable the anticlimax was unbearable for some and they went home. Where there were gaps in my afternoon I played the piano, directing my fingers from the little box in my head labelled 'piano playing' The pathway between that and the broken fingers did its job as always but slowly as if trying out the repair in the machinery. Just at the second finger joint there seemed to be a change of gear and the top two joints moved in slow motion. But they did move and they did play the correct notes eventually. They were very stiff but pain had gone, which was difficult to understand. I kept waiting for pain to flood through me, not be able to carry on, but there was none – just stiffness.

I went home driving the car with one and a half hands and wondering what to say when I got there. I should never have moved the piano. I pulled it over in my frantic hurry to start my teaching day on time. If I didn't I could well have been an hour out by the end of the day. It was typical. I was always in too much of a hurry, always afraid of recrimination

"You're very late tonight"

Why did this casual observation always sound like a question? And why could I never just say "Yes I am" without having to find some explanation. I would explain about traffic, about people being late for lessons as though I had caused all the problems myself. Now as I pulled into the drive I began to rehearse what I would say. The family, two elderly teenagers and a husband were watching television.

"We warmed the casserole and we've had ours. Yours is in the cool oven. It was lovely, we nearly ate it all"

He came into the kitchen to me, the bank paying-in book in his hand. Money first, tea later. The bandages attracted attention.

"What have you done to your hand?"

"I broke it. Well, some of the fingers. The piano fell over"

He arranged all the ten pound notes with the queen at the top right.

"I caught my hand on the hinge as it fell and it cut me. I had to have some stitches"

"How did the piano come to fall over?"

"I kicked it over"

He was writing in the paying in book.

"Someone didn't turn up and I was bored so I went down to the other end of the room, took an almighty run at it and kicked it over. That's all, except that I didn't get out of the way so I broke my hand. Don't worry about it. I should be able to go next week. I just have to check with my own doctor. It's going to be alright."

He had finished filling in my paying in book and closed it. Why did I do that? Why not tell him how devastated I felt about my hand? How it hurt, how I wanted someone to put their arms around me so that I didn't have to be brave any more. More than anything I wanted to weep out all my pain and fear. But I couldn't because I felt so stupid, so incompetent. At least this way I showed that I was dealing with it, that I was taking responsibility for my own stupidity.

"Your tea is in the oven"

He was gone. My hand was throbbing and I felt sick.

"So that, mother, is how I dealt badly with that situation. You see, I was always falling over. The piano didn't fall on me - I pulled it over as *I* fell over. I grasped for something as I fell and it happened to be the piano. That's why I was so apologetic about coming home with my hand broken. It's ridiculous if you think about it for even a minute. I had an accident and all that pain, yet I was driving home worrying about how I should explain it so that I would not appear totally incompetent. Bear in mind, mother, that this is someone who is coming home with the weekly budget".

When the dentist told me I was falling over I knew he was right because of things like this. You can tell anyone they are stupid and incompetent as long as they don't believe they are. But I did believe I was stupid and incompetent because I knew I behaved that way, so I responded by trying to justify my stupidity. If I were not fighting to stay on my feet and had a good 'bite' I would have probably walked in through the door and the scenario would have gone something like this.

"We warmed the casserole… etc" He came into the kitchen after me, paying in book in hand.

"What have you done to your hand?"

"I had an accident today which is the result of the value system we have somehow created and we have to stop it now. I broke my fingers because a piano fell over but this was the result of my panic at leaving my children every week. I am not going to do it any more. The money you are entering at the moment is the last I am going to earn because I am not leaving them any more."

"If only my teeth had come together with more support I might have said it. Hit him over the head with the paying in book even. But it was not to be, mother, for many years. Be satisfied with the progress so far. I have stopped biting my nails and I no longer pull those awful faces as I try to chew inaccessible parts of my cheeks, but I still can't sing and I still never know whether I will be able to cope with the next moment or not".

I got up and left the grave feeling that I had come a long way since sitting on the grass. The evening sun was dipping and the air had a chill. I was not going home. I had rented a small house in London and I was going to open a Voice Workshop, with a climbing frame and space to roll around and discover how the voice really worked. I would offer lessons that included what I was learning about the voice and its links with teeth, jaws and balance on two feet.

Be patient, you have come a long way. You have a way into the information and you just need to keep going. Softly, softly catchy monkey.

"It's you! I don't believe it!
Saw you from across the road.
"Your eldest must be over twenty now,
But you look different-can't put my finger on it"

I kick my shoes off at the door.
The house is empty save for me.
I pour a drink and think about my day,
What was her name?
That woman in the High Street?
Shirley? Cynthia? No, I can't remember
Any more than I remember babies, nappies and prenatal care.
Her name was Yvonne, I remember.
She visits family every weekend, has her Mike
To do repairs, restructuring the garden, replacing window frames..

What shall I have when I am ten years on?
I have this house, this gin and tonic,
Shoes off and time to think.
And that's enough for now.
Will it be then?
Fear grabs me from within,
I teeter, lose my balance, pulled from centre.
Reaching back and forward lose my place.

Get out the mirror, take a look.
Stand on two feet, face smiling, stomach in.
Sing a song or say a poem loud.
Gesticulate to a cheering crowd
Feel the rhythm, feel the sound about your bones.
Make that enough for now.

Yvonne, goodbye. I'll meet my long lost friends
When feet stay on the ground for all encounters.
And when I'm good and ready.

Chapter 14: Recovery

"I know that most men, including those at ease with problems of great complexity, can seldom accept even the simplest and most obvious truth, if it be such as would oblige them to admit the falsity of conclusion which they have delighted in explaining to colleagues, which they have proudly talked to others, and which they have woven into the fabric of their lives" Leo Tolstoy.

I needed a dentist further south if I was to open a Voice Workshop in London, which seemed to be a good idea at the time. My friendly and up to the minute dentist, Joe, was a member of a National Study Group. What better way of meeting dentists than to join the study group myself. Would they have me? I had no medical or dental knowledge or training. I had been reading one of the Group's Journals in Joe's surgery and the articles were full of terms I did not understand with references to anatomy I did not recognise. Supposing I was asked for some sort of accreditation, some level of competence before I could join? After all it was a professional clinical field. How could I show my interest was more than just that of becoming a more informed patient?

There was an advertisement in the Journal. An American dentist called Aelred Fonder was holding a course in Glasgow to discuss his two books – 'The Dental Physician', and 'The Dental Distress Syndrome'. The second title leapt out from the page. Dental distress, that appeared to be what I was suffering from. Quite apart from possibly meeting and talking with members of the group I had to go to hear what this man had to say. It was as much money as a whole term in the Alexander School and I had to stay in the expensive Hotel where the course took place, but I could not afford not to go.

A lone voice teacher among qualified clinicians I listened to reports on case studies just like me, people who were ill in all kinds of different ways, some descending into chronic conditions, all because of the stress imposed on the human system by problems associated with the teeth and the jaw. I began by experiencing yet another enormous feeling of relief that I had discovered this information and these people, for the room was full of dentists from all over the UK, who talked excitedly in the coffee breaks and at the dinner tables. I learned that many were hearing the information for the first time, but all were riveted by it. They had obviously suspected that what they were currently doing for the care of patients was not taking into consideration the effect on the rest of the person's life, but in their training for dentistry they had not been required to look beyond 'the pearly bits'.

The course was three days and on the second day we were given a summary of the events and publications that had changed the thinking of so many clinicians. I discovered that Aelred Fonder's book, 'The Dental Physician' had been in the British Library since 1976, when I was thirty nine. I was born in the thirties before cranial osteopathy was anything but witch craft to most people, including those in the medical profession, and by the same token in the fifties no one may have made a connection between teeth and voices. But why had the training of British dentists since then not included Fonder's information and that of the many other pioneer whole body clinicians? Why had their thinking not expanded the knowledge base so that the dentist who had fitted my bridges also looked at my jaw joint and asked me about my general health to discover whether there were related problem? Was I entering another world with protected boundaries.

When I asked if I could join Cranio Group, as the research group was called, there was surprise at the first interest from a voice teacher, but no refusal. I was given the name of an enlightened dentist in the South, bought 'The Dental Distress Syndrome' and I was ready to begin.

An acrylic shape was moulded to fit over my lower teeth to maintain a space between my back teeth. This would encourage my jaw, which was too far back into the joint, to slide forward and down, hopefully decompressing the two disks of my jaw joint. The appliance was removable, but the message was that the longer I wore it the faster would be the response. Apart from eating, which was impossible with it in place, I wore it all the time.

Meanwhile Camberwell Borough Council provided a hall on an Arts Promotion Scheme with no rent for three months if I offered special community activities. The hall was too big but it fulfilled all other needs. I took it and with someone to take care of the administration and help me set up I began to promote voice and body work while making everyone who came for lessons aware of the importance of questioning their dentist about any proposed treatment plans.

Havill Hall, Camberwell – the first Voice and Body Workshop

A month of free classes was offered to test the water. People coming for a class were astonished to discover that they needed to wear clothes they normally wore in the gym, but it was free so they happily had fun with large inflated balls and walked up and down steps before a mirror to check posture. Then they were to climb while they sang but no one could understand what all this physical exercise had to do with singing. They enjoyed the classes because they were fun and agreed that their singing improved very quickly and surprisingly but the conclusion was always that this was because they were more relaxed. At the end of their freebee they opted for 'proper singing lessons' elsewhere, where you stood beside a piano and sang scales.

I managed to promote the voice and body work through free talks and presentations and although I had this acrylic splint to deal with I could actually speak quite clearly if my tongue articulated my speech much further back in my mouth, so I trained it to do that all the time. I began to smile very broadly and talk like a ventriloquist. In my naivety and enthusiasm for promoting this new area of self development I thought it would be powerful to explain that I was wearing this bizarre lump of plastic in order to discover how to get my voice back to its original beauty and range and it was all part of the work at the Voice Workshop. At the end of each session my audience fled, not even wanting to join with me in discussion.

Not deterred I arranged for the dentist I was working with to come to the workshop and give a talk on the importance of considering what your jaw may be doing to your life if it needed some correction. I advertised widely in London but only about twelve turned up. Like me the dentist was also very enthusiastic and used one of the audience, with her permission, to illustrate what was meant by a clicking jaw. Permission was withdrawn the moment he described her problem. She defended her 'click' as nothing at all according to her own dentist, while she described his diagnosis as 'touting for work'. She left immediately and the evening dragged to a sad close with a row of stony faces daring anyone to notice anything else.

Two months later, still with money slipping away week by week and no work, I nevertheless had an amazing opening to my mouth. The dentist decided to make me a dental plate to replace teeth at the back of my bottom jaw although he might have put the Bolder Dam in my mouth for all I knew. I hadn't had any teeth at the back of my lower jaw for thirty years and the soft tissue had taken up the shrunken dimension. I began to learn about whole body dentistry, not from the courses, not from books, but right where it was happening. Within two days I could hardly drag myself out of bed; I ached in every limb. By mid day I had to go home to sleep, my whole head throbbing and my body wracked with exhaustion. When I took out the plate the discomfort stopped everywhere as if by magic but I determined to persevere. I was obviously stretching muscle tissue and sometime it must stretch and the pain would go. When I returned to the dentist he filed bits off the denture in an effort to make it comfortable but nothing made it comfortable.

After a month I seemed to have got used to a low level of pain so I stopped my visits to the dentist while I brought in some money doing workshops for school teachers who were losing their voices. For the first time I met people who were enthusiastic about what I was doing. None of the school teachers had received any voice training to enter a profession that was totally dependant upon having a good reliable voice.

This was another revelation for me and when I looked at the way they stood, and the way they sang I was sure I could help these teachers with their voices.

"I need to learn to project my voice"

"My breathing is not very good when I teach. I run out of breath. I need to learn to breathe deeper."

"I need more confidence"

"No, I never sing. I sang in infant school but then I was turned down for the choir, so I knew I couldn't sing. I've never bothered since"

They took to the voice and body work like ducks to water. They admitted that although they knew that all learning was accelerated by an element of play, present teaching policies left little room or time for it and they had generally lost sight of this fundamental educational principle. At last, a direction to go in. After several successful in-service training days I persuaded an area manager of schools to attend a day of my exercise programme for teachers. He watched a morning in which thirty teachers from junior schools skipped, stretched and exercised while singing and reciting to connect voice and body. They were all laughing and having fun while they learned how the voice actually worked as opposed to how they had believed it did and experiencing the resonance of the voice throughout their whole body. They so enjoyed finding their own voices. The man who had booked me for this course dropped in.

Demonstrating Voice and Body exercise

"This is very interesting and they are obviously having fun, which is good for relaxation, but what teachers really need is to learn to project the voice".

"The voice does not 'project'. They are learning to be a resonating chamber for the sound they make. This is what turns their own small sound into a voice that will fill a classroom with resonance and quality. You work on posture and flexibility to create that".

"Unfortunately our funding is limited to producing a direct result. At the end of the day they do need to project".

I was taught to 'project' my voice. The more people I saw sing in performance and speak in classrooms and public arenas the more I saw the results of my own training at Music College. The more I observed, the more obvious became the paradigm for 'having a voice' in singing or in speech. I wrote down what I saw.

- Speaking or singing over a distance always began with taking a good breath, usually in through the mouth. This was accompanied by bracing the legs.
- The face became impassive and stern reminding me of the 'take that smile off your face and get on with your work' attitude to concentration.
- The performance conveyed nothing; no story, no passion for the telling, no personal involvement, no playing of the instrument to suit the audience.
- The tongue was obviously very flat in the mouth throughout.
- The whole performance was nervous and stressful for both performer and listener.

There was a much bigger problem here than I had ever realised. I had assumed that things had moved on from the teaching I had experienced thirty years ago; that I would turn up with my experimental voice and body work to be greeted by those who had already made changes to the training and were now more experienced in it than I; that I would be able to learn from the present up to date voice teachers as I was learning from the up to date dentists. But no one seemed to understand what I was doing.

I sent leaflets to all Music Colleges and Theatres in London. My approach was to introduce the importance of voice and body maintenance to a career in professional performance by learning appropriate exercise and knowing what questions to ask your dentist so that he didn't do inappropriate work on your teeth. No working singers, students or teachers ever came to investigate my workshop, even from curiosity. However I did get a number of people who could not sing at all, or who hated their own voice. I expect they thought that bouncing around on big balls and climbing while reading was enough of a distraction to combat the terror they had of their own voices. These activities reduced the amount of air they breathed in, loosened their legs, improved their posture and introduced right brain thinking. They began to 'play' their voice and their voices and their confidence improved. They began to sing enjoyably and in tune. This was not about relaxation. It was about the need to work in a more appropriate and efficient way to empower yourself.

It occurred to me that from what I had learned in my college singing lessons I would never have been able to teach someone how to sing who couldn't. What would my professor have done with someone who could not sing? That was not a problem. He would never have met such a person. They did not exist for him. Neither did they exist for me until I lost my own ability to sing. Before that I too thought that singing was a talent I had and others didn't. At the end of my training I gained a diploma to teach singing but if someone had asked me to teach them because they didn't sing but would love to I would have been totally inept, wouldn't have known where to start. Imagine ringing up a teacher of French and asking for lessons.

"I want to speak French. I have always been fascinated by the culture and the sound of the language. I listen to people speaking French and long for the resonance in my own voice that seems to be created just by that language; that singing sultry inflection. I see from the yellow pages that you are a teacher of French. I would like to book some lessons and learn to speak the language"

"I will book a first lesson for you, which will be an audition. I will ask you to read some French to see whether I think it is worth your carrying on. You don't want to spend money if I am not going to be able to help you. How much French have you spoken before?"

We all have singing as part of our speech process if we belong to the species Homo Sapiens. The *singing* part of that process is much older than our ability to speak. Set us down in the jungle and we will hear all the sounds the human voice has inherited. However, it is unlikely you will hear "Pass me those pliers" because only Homo Sapiens has speech, due to the development of upright posture, the cerebral cortex of the brain, the right angled position of the tongue and the low larynx. So, we do not talk like Daleks, we use pitch to express language. We all sing every time we speak, even if it is over a small pitch range and a tune out of our own heads. All a singing teacher has to do is take our own speech and stretch it into a bigger pitch range, give us this basic information and the confidence to use it. Nothing could be easier. How could I gain a diploma for teaching singing without knowing that? It meant that I was really no good to anyone who couldn't sing, which appeared to be the majority of the white British population, in contrast to other ethnic cultures where music and singing seemed to be important.

It was inevitable that one day someone with influence who couldn't sing would learn to sing in my workshop, recognise the benefit and talk about it at work. I received a call from TV's 'This Morning'. Would I go to Liverpool and take a phone in on the programme hosted by Richard and Judy? Wow! This was the spring board to fame and getting the information out there.

If I found a public voice I could air the increasing problems encountered by those who practiced whole body dentistry via post graduate training available from America or Australia. The General Dental Council, realising that this training encouraged the fitting of appliances in the mouth to expand facial bone structure, saw it as an entry by dentists into orthodontics, without the necessary certification. This was bringing the 'whole body' dentists into conflict with their professional authority. It was also a medical paradigm that beyond the mid teens cranial bones did not move and so expansion of the dental arches, seen by my colleagues as a preferable alternative to the extraction of teeth for crowded mouths, was becoming a dental battleground.

The TV programme provided me with a climbing frame and space to introduce my physio-balls into the sofa area, generally only for lounged chatting. The whole TV slot went like a dream and there was unprecedented response to the phone in, Richard sat on a ball and did the exercises, I climbed and sang, which still gave me the best of my voice.

It was April 1st, and my slot in the programme was screened in the morning. Viewers rang in to say that after becoming riveted to the screen by identifying with information on their own voices they then realised it was the best April fool trick that ITV had yet staged.

Chapter 15: A Fellow Traveller

I now understood why my workshop was not working, probably never would. The concept of paying attention to the balance and posture of the body was new and like John Harrison's clock that eventually solved the longitude problem, no one would take it on board and try it out. I had wanted to improve voice training because I had not benefited from mine but there were countless books on voice improvement and singing and they all said the same things. The ground rules were set and there were many eminent teachers prepared to defend them. Any body work encountered during voice training was not part of the individual voice lessons but separate lessons in the Alexander Technique, which ignored structures like teeth and jaws. It was down to the students of voice to put it all together and discover structural problems themselves. The danger was that they would discover them by the same process I had, by developing these problems themselves. There seemed no way to get this information in at the beginning of training, or better still into schools and into parents.

I could not go on with this. There were so many areas that I could see must somehow affect each other. The loss of my voice, which was still a very difficult emotional area for me to deal with; what the dentists were learning about whole body dentistry; the problems I could see around me in the way the voice was used by almost everyone. Beyond the clinicians no one seemed ready to believe there was any connection. Certainly no one in singing, the very area I found most difficult to approach. Any integration of all this information was beyond me, my finances and my courage.

I had one more month in my little house and then I would have to move as I could no longer pay the rent. I had spent most of my divorce settlement getting this far and this far was nowhere. Money must come in and I had only one more workshop.

I packed my travelling circus of balance boards, physio-balls, large wall charts of texts to read from, song sheets, stretch bands, beanbags to throw and rhythm balls to bounce to music, asking myself all the while the things I had been asked ever since I began this nightmare.

"What has all this to do with singing? People *do* just stand up and sing and other people see them as talented, musical and confident. In spite of this struggle I still couldn't sing and maybe there were people whose voices *did* fail for natural reasons of age and general inadequacy. All the books on singing emphasized the spiritual, emotional and intellectual training of the voice. All the books emphasized the need for a flat tongue to open the throat. All the books taught you to breathe correctly and 'drop your jaw', all the things I had been told. Had I failed for the reasons I was given – stress, emotional instability? Was I really mad after all?"

This was a workshop for stammerers. What was I doing here? This was not my field. I knew nothing about stammering. Was this the final indication that I was totally out of my depth? After this weekend I would begin to look for teaching jobs, school music teaching jobs. Get back where you belong and do something useful that earns you a living.

There were thirty people in the workshop, of which only three were women. Past caring whether anyone argued with me I demonstrated the changes in the voice due to changes in posture and balance. We stretched and bounced on physio balls while reading and singing and everyone became very excited when it was discovered that I was right – there were changes in the voice afterwards, and all for the better. It's a strange phrase "My stammer improved when I did that" It would seem to indicate that the stammer got worse, but certainly the room was becoming more vocal and the voices were becoming clear and more fluent. I had found the first people who were willing to play with their voices and in spite of always considering myself vocally fluent in speech and singing I felt strangely at home. Was I also a stammerer? I learned that weekend that many people are covert stammerers and that stammerers do not stammer when they sing. But maybe I did. Certainly I had all the fear of using my voice in singing that dogged the stammerer in speech. What I did that afternoon was so interesting to them I was asked to remain for the second day, meet the group socially and answer questions.

As I watched my six male dinner companions struggle to speak to me I saw various contortions of the jaw and face muscles. I discovered that all six held responsible positions requiring a high degree of skill and management, a museum curator, the head of an engineering company, an expert in whole body vibration injury. For all of them stammering had begun around four to five years old. I was sure that in my own case it was the desire and consequent struggle to sing in spite of the limited and uneven movement of my jaw that had compounded my distress and finally lost me my peace of mind. Could the same happen to a small child who was exceptionally bright and struggling to express a myriad of thoughts and ideas through a mechanical system that trapped and prevented the child getting it all out without a struggle. Where would that struggle go? Would it go into forcing the words past that restricted space that was around the jaw? Would the muscles finally go into the kind of spasm that I could see in the men around the table and block the speech process? Was I looking at jaw related voice problems?

All were interested in the concept of the body being responsible for the efficiency of the voice as this was entirely new. None of their years of speech therapy, hypnotherapy, cognitive therapy, confidence counselling or even shiatsu, which they had experienced on this weekend, had mentioned or worked on a connection between what happened in speech and what happened in their posture or body behaviour, still less, their jaws. Any body work was for relaxation as it was generally considered that stammerers were 'stressed'. One remained long after the bar had finally closed and stripped all my precariously connected information down to the bone. As I told him how I had discovered it he said,

"You're a researcher like me".

I also explained that I had to give it up and forget it, go back into mainstream teaching to earn my living.

"You should write this up before you do that. Write a paper and submit it to a conference. You are interested in the jaws and teeth of stammerers, do it properly. Get a dentist to examine a group of stammerers. If anything interesting comes out of it do a pilot study, then write a paper for the next Dysfluency Conference. Goodnight, see you tomorrow".

Just like that! The last academic effort for me was an A level essay on Chaucer's Wife of Bath. I went to bed. After the questions the next morning I drove home and planned the move.

While I was agonizing over re-entering a world of information I knew was obsolete I received a package of papers, references and book extracts from my friendly scientist, whose name was Chris. He had walked in the Welsh Brecon Hills and deliberately lowered his back pack to add weight to his pelvis, encouraging a lower centre of gravity because this is what I had talked about in relation to the work on the physio balls and the balance boards. He then sang and recited all the way uphill, discovering both a lower and more resonant voice and afterwards in the pub, greater fluency. Although he lost this fluency very quickly it had twitched his nose for research and he was concerned that I may give up what I was doing.

What is it that sends people into our lives? I had the story but could not tell it to the people who needed to know. Selected and received wisdom supported the argument for the status quo, the vocal paradigm that existed. All the books, all the research in voice so far justified the need to increase the volume and pressure of air in order to produce the voice. All the books pointed to voice problems beginning with stress that was psychologically or emotionally triggered. Music was thought to be in the mind and in the genes, not in physical or environmental development. I could stand up and passionately beat the drum of change, but I would never change anything because I did not know how to penetrate the system. That needed an objective, scientific approach that could set aside passion in order to win the argument. Chris was to teach me how to write up my discoveries with objectivity and precision so they could be presented through conference publications and articles.

While this was encouraging it was to take some years to train me to think and write this clearly and meanwhile I was losing faith in my dentist. Whatever he adjusted caused more pain in my mouth and stiffness in my body. I knew he was wrestling with new techniques and feeling his way but I had only one life and that seemed to be flagging. I had been so sure that my problems were due to the Dental Distress Syndrome, but I was exhausted with it all and losing my way.

My treatment of the very obvious jaw and bite problem had been ongoing for more than a year and I was now in continuous pain and my voice was not responding to the changes. Also I was beginning to experience difficulty in using balance boards, something that had been easy at the beginning of treatment. The lump sum from the sale of my half of the house had gone with nothing achieved. The rest of my settlement from the divorce was to be paid quarterly for five years but there were now only two years left. I took the dental plate out of my mouth and went to ground for a month to lick my wounds. I needed to think what to do next.

After two very black weeks my dentist rang with a last ditch suggestion. A course was to be given by an Australian called Bob Walker, who was both dentist and a cranial chiropractor. The course was called 'Chirodontics' to cover both disciplines. It was for a team of a dentist and a cranial chiropractor or cranial osteopath and the course addressed the emerging problem of recognising the jaw's relationship, not only with the skull, but with the rest of the balance and function of the body. Many dentists were seeing obvious jaw problems and treating them without realising that what they saw were only symptoms. The actual problem was elsewhere in the body, often in asymmetry of the cranial bones, which had been misaligned, probably in the birth process. The suggestion was that this asymmetry had to be fixed first *before* tackling any problems of jaw or teeth.. My dentist was eager to discover any improvement possibilities and decided that the team he took should include me, as a patient to be discussed.

The displacement of the bones of the skull during the birth process is not generally considered significant. Cranial osteopaths and cranial chiropractors do not agree with this general view. They encourage all new births to be checked within two or three weeks to ensure that the infant skull has recovered from the pressure of the birth process. However it is generally believed the skull bones, plastic at birth to allow passage through the pelvic girdle, recover from this pressure, grow together and eventually fuse in a developmental pattern that naturally corrects any minor deformities caused at birth.

My dentist, in good faith, had lined my jaw up in relation to my skull assuming that the skull was a good reference for 'level'. When lines were drawn on my face it was clear that the two sides were not at all the same level By correcting my jaw to the level of my lopsided cheekbones, the dentist had actually added to my problem. The plate was painful because it was pushing me even further into dental distress.

How are you supposed to discover anything at all without doing the wrong thing at least half of the time? The information on the role of the teeth and jaw in the efficient and effortless working of the whole system was new and experimental. I was beginning to realise how ignorant and stuck I was about information that vitally affected my life. I really knew nothing about my own workings. I had always accepted what the dentist, the doctor and the teacher said and had learned nothing about myself except what I had learned from them. Here I was, finally filling in this void in my education at all of fifty five. I had spent most of my life in dumb acceptance of information from those I considered were my betters.

The only one who had tested my sense of personal responsibility had been the Australian doctor in A&E when I broke my hand. He was here in the UK. for just a year to learn surgical techniques, but usually worked in the Australian outback, where self recovery was paramount and you only

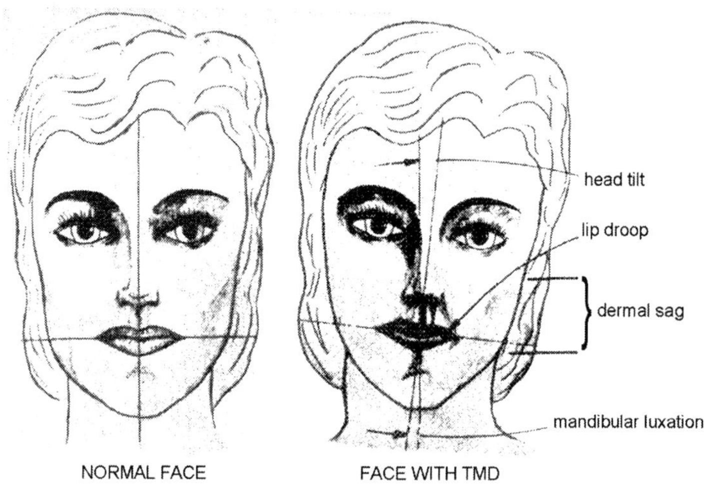

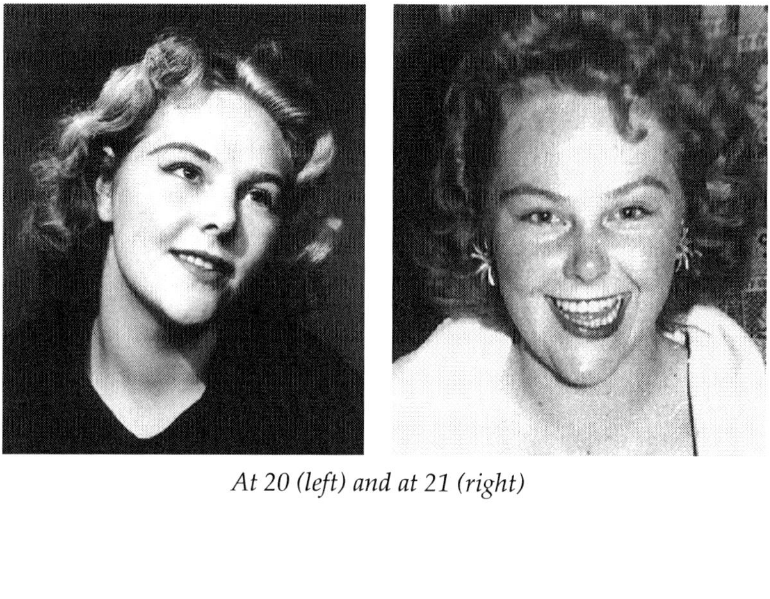

At 20 (left) and at 21 (right)

called the doctor if you absolutely could not get up on your horse. He gave me *all* the information, not what I should know that was convenient for *him*.

The jaw joints are in the two paired temporal bones, which were out of alignment in my skull. One jaw joint was forward and the other back, as were my eyes, my ears and my cheekbones. The plate needed to come out and we would have to begin all over again correcting first the result of the birth trauma; literally straightening me up. My poor bite was not initially a dental problem but a cranial one although gradually over the years my jaw had modified to this contorted pattern. The whole bone structure of my upper jaw – my maxilla – the bone that made up the front of my face, needed expanding where it had collapsed due to the extractions in my twenties. It seemed impossible that the front of my face could be changed at sixty which is where I was now, and made to grow to accommodate teeth that would be fitted into the new space, but I was assured that bones move or develop because they are stimulated in some way to do so and with persistence all can change.

We were talking another two years at least but I felt strong again and ready to tackle putting it right The additional information from the chirodontist had finally completely explained the link between my birth and the subsequent jaw problem and put me back on track.

The importance of interaction between clinical disciplines was beginning to emerge. Maybe a new humility was needed at a high level of medical skill to open the way to more lateral thinking and discussion with experts outside one's own field. I sat down and wrote the story for myself, point by point while it was clear in my head:

1. I had suffered birth trauma that had left my paired temporal bones out of line with one another
2. Throughout childhood my jaw, which jointed on each side with the two offset temporal bones gradually skewed, making it impossible for my developing teeth to line up
3. I gradually lost my balance on two feet.
4. However, I had this terrific childhood full of play and stimulation with parents who believed in children doing things

rather than staying clean. My imagination was tested at every turn and I was expected to take some responsibility within the family from being quite young.

5. Then there was the music. It requires symmetry and balance to play an instrument and sing. Did I instinctively recognise that playing the piano relieved the distress I must have already been experiencing at a level beyond my consciousness? Did I love to play and sing, or did I need to play and sing. And if I had not played so much and achieved the standard I did, would anyone have remembered the Wizard and connected the two?

6. My magic childhood and subsequent schooling provided the stability and security that I lacked in myself so that by fifteen I was a high achiever.

7. It is reckoned that it takes about fifteen years from the moment of damage to run out of the 'Adaptive Range' of compensating for it. For me that was in my sixth form, aged 15-16 when I could no longer write the essays even though my head understood the concepts. I ducked out and went to study singing. Was my voice merely the last ability to break down because being built into the breathing system it draws on the most fundamental compensatory system? We are programmed to stay alive, and breathing makes this possible.

With the interdisciplinary effort of not one but two clinicians I was confident I would not only get my singing back but quality of life as well.

I now ran all newfound information past Chris, my friendly scientist. Oh the joy to be able to open the floodgates and voice ones own ideas without them being judged as nonsense simply because no one appeared to have thought of it before. To pick through the mess in one's brain with someone schooled in clear sightedness and clarity of thought. Being steeped in scientific academia he could have been excessively left brained, but this was tempered by a love of music, poetry, cooking and Lovelock's 'Gaia' view of the world. My predominantly right brained outlook was tempered by a Victorian upbringing, where structure and rules formed a background to daily life. As I talked through what I understood and what I didn't I saw how much I had hidden for fear of total discouragement. His upbringing had not encouraged the discussion of feelings, following one's instinct or awareness of body intelligence. It was perhaps inevitable that we would grow to need, support and complement one another.

He taught me to write clearly, objectively and with no personal opinion. The changes in my thinking were as painful as the changes to my structure but just as necessary if mind and body were to jointly recover. I had lost my love of schooling and learning by the time I was sixteen. I could have supported my father's insistence on my staying in school to complete my A levels, but I couldn't cope with the work. Now I knew that by then I was running out of the ability to compensate for the torsion in my body that increased year by year until it limited my potential and the space in my mouth that would have housed my wisdom teeth. I just needed to start learning from where I left off at sixteen.

I moved the Voice and Body Centre into the first floor of his house. We turned one room into an office and the largest room into a mini gym with a climbing frame on one wall, a hanging bar and large texts of poems and songs. Armed with my stretch bands, physio balls and balance boards I once again advertised voice and body exercise. Again the clients were mainly those who suffered from continual voice problems, but I had long accepted that if I were to discover how to improve voices this is where I must begin. I now had sympathetic colleagues in Cranio Group and when I recognised problems in the jaw or posture too severe to be corrected by my own exercises I referred the client to a voice-aware dentist, cranial osteopath or cranial chiropractor. Interdisciplinary correction of voice problems had begun.

A last my own treatment was working. As a result of the cranial chiropractic my temporal bones and consequently cheek bones became level and this levelled my eyes and my ears. The dentist could now begin to correct my bite by relating my jaw to this new level, but the original bridges had to go. They were maintaining the uneven position against my now level upper teeth. Wire expansion appliances were inserted in the upper and lower arches of my teeth and once again my tongue position changed, now operating continuously even further back against my palate. I began to breathe through my nose with an efficiency I had never experienced before. The continual grinding action of nail biting and cheek chewing had worn down all my remaining teeth, so the decision was made to crown all of my front upper teeth, insert new bridges in the now much bigger spaces and increase the height of my bite. This involved making the teeth for the upper crowns and bridges longer, then fitting metal plates (brackets) on all of my teeth and connecting upper and lower teeth with elastics. When I opened my mouth I pulled on the lower teeth and gradually they erupted from the jaw bone. My face began to fill out and lose its hard, drawn look. It was easier to smile and at last I had something to smile about.

I was gradually coming level and my voice was responding too. I knew from the balance board work that my weight had shifted but now my right hip began to hurt every time I put my foot to the floor. An X- ray revealed that a life of unbalanced walking had worn away some of the surface cartilage from the bone and the hip joint would need surgical intervention to prevent total breakdown.

The consultation with the orthopaedic surgeon of the local hospital took me back thirty years. I was shown in to the consulting room by a nurse and waited while the consultant examined my X-ray. Then he finally spoke to me for the first time.

"You need a hip joint replacement. We will put you on the list"

There was no explanation, no gentle introduction to a major surgical procedure but this time I was different. No more giving responsibility for my treatment into the hands of someone whose competence was unknown to me.

"May I ask some questions about that?"

"What do you want to know? "

"What are the benefits from this operation?"

He looked surprised.

"I can see from your walk that you are in pain. Afterwards you will be walking pain free. What more do you need?"

"But I understand this operation has a limited time for success, about ten to fifteen years and that a great deal of bone is removed. That would mean that at seventy I may be looking at the same operation again, only with reduced bone mass. I have spent years trying to rebalance myself on two feet by correcting a severe jaw problem. I teach voice and body work that requires me to twist and rotate. Will that still be possible?"

I could see that I had lost his attention. He was reading notes on his desk.

"I would think" and he paused to remove the phrase "at your age" from the tape, but it crackled in the air, "you would be grateful to be pain free and able to walk"

"For me that is not enough. Is there an alternative procedure?"

"There is no proven alternative with any successful track record that I can recommend"

His voice was becoming hard around the edges and I recognised that my voice used to be the one to do this in such circumstances.

"I need to go away and think. I also need to try to find some other way that allows me to do what I do".

"You are obviously not yet in enough pain. You'll be back when you are."

How I had changed. How I would have cowed and apologised in my twenties, thirties or forties. How I would have lost my way in the exchange, probably cried and acquiesced. Now I left thinking only that I would go under a bus if the pain became unbearable rather than allow this man to wield any power over me whatsoever.

While I hunted for an answer I conducted the suggested pilot study on stammerers for a European Conference on Dysfluency. A dentist, a physiotherapist and I examined 32 stammerers and discovered TMD – Temporo Mandibular Dysfunction and musculo-skeletal torsion in all of them and we all went to Munich to deliver a combined presentation. It was an exercise in teaching me to write and present a paper. My stupidity to manage a computer had to be seen to be believed but it gave me confidence as our findings confirmed that voice problems were accompanied by and may be caused by problems not generally associated with the voice.

On one of my trips to collect data I picked up the Telegraph to read on the train and found an article about Jonah Barrington, World Squash Champion, whose career was cut short by arthritis in the hip. He returned to the game after an operation developed in the UK by Mr Derek McMinn, an orthopaedic surgeon at the Royal Orthopaedic Hospital in Birmingham. It had a successful track record of seven years and without removing any bone, resurfaced the hip joint. The result was strength in every twist and rotation.

I contacted Mr McMinn's secretary and discovered that of the few surgeons in the UK trained to carry out this operation one was local. Within two weeks of a consultation I was taken into a private hospital and my hip was resurfaced. This was obviously the procedure the NHS consultant was unable to recommend because of a limited track record. I had to pay for it myself from a business loan.

I was only out of action for a month as one of the conditions for the success of the 'athletic' hip operation is to recover range of movement as quickly as possible, which I thoroughly understood from the recovery of my piano playing after the broken hand. I resisted the temptation to return to the hospital consultant and tell him. My behaviour was changing. I had become confident and did not need to return to negative situations. I was on two feet with a wide smile and my teeth were together when I closed them

Paradoxically when I had been falling over I lacked any support at all, either inside me or in the world around. Now I was on two feet and felt no fear of falling I had help, support and love. And because I was secure in myself I could love someone back. It was all a joy and a revelation to be in this secure world I recognised dimly from childhood but had not known since. I am not so naïve as to believe the people around me had changed. I had changed and it allowed me to behave differently, not feel threatened and defensive. I was no longer driving people away.

My music began to come back, tentatively at first as though afraid of another beating. I noticed it first in my piano playing. Since the accident to my hand I had always assumed that I would have limited facility; my acute ear recognised the slower scale passages and not-quite-on–the–moment rhythm. Now those boundaries were gone and I played more accurately. My music had begun with the piano and I sang after I learned to play. The pattern repeated itself now. I played and played until I was really enjoying playing again without any 'what ifs'. One day I just wanted to sing and so I did. There was much work to do, but the feel was different; secure within, like me.

Chris and I decided this was a good time to get married. It seemed to be naturally the next step.

My true love hath my heart and I have his,
I keep his in a jar upon the shelf
"How can I justify this gift" I ask my love
My love replies "Just be yourself"

My true love hath my heart and I have his,
He keeps mine amidst piles of other things
Bike chain, scissors, various tools.
Amid the mess he comes upon my heart, and smiles.

My true love hath my heart and I have his,
We've nothing else of one another, want no more
Of one another, will not use one another
To make ourselves secure.

My true love hath my heart and I have his,
We're surely not in love, this can't be love.
Experience of love is pain and tears,
Fear, doubt, defence and insecurity.

My true love hath my heart and I have his,
Whenever we're together life is fun.
We laugh a lot, and everything is easy,
Sans time, sans place, sans age, sans everything.

Chapter 16: Teaching Differently

The internet was becoming a powerful tool for extending public knowledge and consequently public choice. The hip resurfacing operation that was not offered to me by the consultant as an option had been discovered in the daily newspaper, but the information that influenced my choice was on a website. There I could read about the development of the operation, the mistakes, breakthroughs, changes of material and planning. By the time I had read all the information available I felt I knew Mr McMinn and recognised the passion for his sure knowledge that this operation could work. That gave me the confidence to make a decision to have the resurfacing operation.

I wanted to let young singers know what had happened to me because I had dumbly accepted that anyone who taught me singing must know what they were talking about. I had not yet worked out why this was so, why I mindlessly took on board, for instance, training my tongue to stay in the floor of my mouth without asking

"Where did you get this information? Where can I read about it and check it for myself?"

My piano teachers never held me in such thrall. Was this because the singing teacher deals with an instrument that is never kept safely in its case? The song you sing this morning in this lesson may reflect the murmurings in your lover's ear last night, or the hurt you feel at the letter you have just received. Does that excessively add to the vulnerability already present in the playing of music? Does that give the singing teacher extraordinary powers over you?

I needed a comprehensive website with information about the links between voice problems and dental problems, the effect of extraction of teeth on the development of the face and 21st Century whole body dentistry. Teachers and singers would find it and be informed. We called the site The Voice and Body Centre. I wrote everything I knew and Chris formatted and designed the site. I was invited to write articles by editors who found the site and we were soon adding information from other disciplines interested in working with voices. We put in links pages to a national network of dentists, cranial chiropractors and cranial osteopaths who would offer help to worried musicians and we were soon adding relevant articles, pictures and research papers. I stopped advertising myself as a singing teacher, which attracted those whose aim was to win competitions and collect exam successes, and waited for those who were interested in this new direction of teaching of the co-ordination of voice and body to contact me.

We were in a University town and the first contact was an invitation to teach singing students from the performance course of the University Music Department. These were the first singers I had taught since discovering the role my jaw had played in my own singing and I saw this as a relief from the clinical aspects of singing and an opportunity to step back into music and teach young developing singers with no problems. I thought the chance of finding a singer with the results of a severe birth trauma was pretty remote as they all required a Grade 8 examination success before singing could be their chosen instrument and anyway, there were only eight of them. I enthusiastically set about extending their range of material and began stretch exercises and balance work.

After the first month two of the girls began to miss lessons. They had colds, then flu and were always excessively tired. I continued to concentrate on their singing until I discovered that the University Health Clinic had prescribed antidepressants for 'the emotional stress of being at University' and given them a couple of weeks off to take the medication and recover. I could no longer ignore their narrow faces and limited mouth opening and discovered that both had had premolars removed for overcrowded mouths at around fourteen years old.

The removal of the premolar teeth, two at the top and two at the bottom is standard procedure in NHS dentistry when the arches of the teeth are too small for the number of second teeth that appear. Count four from the middle top or bottom, the middle being one, to find the premolars if you still have them; there should be a matching pair of teeth on each side. With four teeth extracted there is more space for the rest and they can be pulled into a beautiful even smile with the aid of tram tracks; metal brackets cemented to each tooth and joined by a wire that pulls the whole arch of teeth into line. This seems a reasonable enough way to deal with both a ragged smile and teeth that do not meet in a bite, unless you question why the teeth crowd in the first place. Obviously the arch is too small, but why is it too small? All your teeth have been in your skull from about four years old, so why has the bone not developed enough?

The genetic factor is important – we do look like our parents and it is possible that with two children in a family, one can be wide faced and one narrow faced because of different genetic heritage, but thumb sucking can slow down face development, and children who do not work their breathing system hard by skipping, jumping, climbing and singing may also have long narrow faces. Also the modern Western soft diet is creating narrow dental arches as form is dictated by function. But for whatever reason a narrow maxilla (front of the face and roof of the mouth) does not happen overnight. At seven or eight it becomes apparent that the arch is not developing well, so why not do something about it then, when bones are very plastic and only need a little encouragement to develop more, and more quickly.

If I could have both arches successfully expanded at fifty five and maintain the space with bridges, imagine how easily a child of seven or eight could gain the space into which all the teeth would eventually beautifully and evenly slot. As in my own case the removal of teeth causes the bones of the face, already narrow, to narrow still further, interfering with the way the tongue articulates in the mouth. A naturally sized tongue will not fit up into an unnaturally narrow roof of the mouth, it falls down flat. Face muscles designed to stretch the face wide around the eyes cease to operate when the tongue is flat in the mouth and over time the face continues to develop a long narrow shape with a long narrow nose ill-equipped for breathing. Was the breathing and consequently the health of these two girls being affected by the narrowing of their faces that the premolar extractions had caused?

I decided that two did not prove anything, especially against the might of orthodontic received wisdom, which would have us believe that any expansion of the bone structure is likely to regress in the long term. I couldn't imagine how a voice teacher could even get to ask the questions on that one. Nevertheless I introduced exercises that would encourage the tongue to work harder against the palate, hopefully increasing the widening of the face with sheer muscle power.

As each new intake of singers appeared at the beginning of the academic year it became more difficult for me to ignore the underdevelopment of their voices even though all had achieved advanced examination certificates for singing. . No one seemed to know how to open the mouth. All were driving their jaws back into the joint instead of allowing the jaw to slide forward and down. I asked how they believed they should open their mouths and the answer was always.

"I must drop my jaw"

Where had I heard that before?

"What about your tongue. What do you know about that?"

"I need to keep the tip touching the front of my bottom teeth to open my throat to sing".

I knew now from working with the radical dentists and experimenting with myself, that a flat tongue forced the jaw back into the joint when the mouth was opened. Was it possible that the same information I was taught forty years ago was still being taught, that nothing had changed?

I gave them all the exercises I had done myself to reposition the tongue further back in the mouth. Except in four students the jaw problems went away as the tongue moved back and the jaw moved forward. Those four had had premolars removed in their teens, including the two girls who regularly missed work through illness, and none of these tongues would fit into the palate. The singers thought the tongue was too big. I thought the palate was too small and I was forced to say so.

These young minds questioned and probed, coming in before a lesson to read my books and papers on the new possibilities in dentistry and the choices which were available but never given to the public. I had not sought this complication to what should have been an enjoyable development of young musical skill, but I could not deny what I saw when questioned. One girl decided to visit a cranial osteopath and on his advice her parents took her to the dentist he worked with. She appeared in the department all wired up to expand her upper arch and pull her jaw forward.

It was time for another pilot study, this time for a Voice Conference. I had only so far considered that insensitive or out of date dentistry could damage the voices of those who already sang. Now I was horrified by the prospect that a young voice could be limited by removing the premolars or by receiving out of date information on voice mechanics and never develop singing at all. As I embarked upon writing the paper such a voice walked in. He was eighteen, round-faced and pudgy. He was a first year student, not a singer but a double bass player.

"I know I can sing. I could sing until I was fifteen, I took an active part in National Youth Music Theatre. Then my voice just went almost overnight and now I can't sing at all so I play the double bass instead. I had a consultation with a laryngologist who looked at my vocal cords. There's nothing wrong with my voice. I had looked at your website so I asked for an appointment with an orthodontist because I've had my premolars removed. He says there is no connection. Everyone says it is stress…the fear of not being able to sing makes it happen. I *know* I can sing and I want to be a singer, not a bass player".

Years ago, when I taught singing by teaching scales and songs; when I sat at the piano listening to the voice that stood opposite me repeating voice exercises a semitone higher until the voice wouldn't go any further; when I classified singers as sopranos or mezzos, tenors and basses according to how high or how low they could sing I was invited to join the British Association of Teachers of Singing. I went along to hear the chairman wind up their Annual Conference. To end his talk he told the story of someone ringing up to ask for a consultation lesson because she wanted to study something particular. Impressed by this he made the appointment and the singer entered carrying a score of Puccini's 'Madame Butterfly'. When he asked which bit she wanted to work on she said she didn't know, she had only just bought the score because she heard it, knew that it was what she wanted to sing and somewhere inside herself, knew she could. The conference erupted with laughter. His parting shot was

"We have all met someone like that in our teaching, someone whose aspirations are well beyond their talent. My message is that you will survive these people and carry on doing the splendid work you are all doing. Good afternoon and a safe journey home!"

I was not inspired to join.

I remembered the woman who stood up in the Music Festival in Leamington Spa and always sang the same aria grossly out of tune.

Everyone slid down in their seat when she appeared, but she ploughed through the aria year after year. Why did she? Was she totally insensitive or was her agony much greater than ours? Was she asking for help in the only way she knew and were we all crucifying her by not recognising what the pain really was about?

Do we listen to the crippling messages that doom us to failure before we begin or do we listen to the poet Robert Browning who said…

"Man's aim should exceed his grasp, or what's a heaven for?"

Did these people who sang so badly know what we singing teachers didn't? That they could sing what they said they could and we were too dumb or maybe too arrogant to unlock their potential and our egos prevented us from learning how?

This young man's premolars were removed when he was fourteen and the bone structure reduced to an acceptable smile. By now it was so obvious to me that this limited the voice but I could only say,

"My opinion is that you will only sing if the bone structure of your maxilla and your jaw are both expanded and the premolar teeth put back. No one else is likely to tell you this. I know of no orthodontist who has ever put the premolars back, so there's no track record to give you. I don't know whether it can be done or what the effect will be. I can't give you assurance of anything. This procedure is new, experimental and you have to pay for it because the NHS doesn't recommend the expansion techniques you will have to undergo. You will be told by most orthodontists licensed by the British Orthodontic Society that any expansion of your dental arches will regress. When I consider what you will have to take on I think the best thing would be for you to carry on playing your bass".

He still wanted to discuss it with the dentist who was treating me and by his first appointment he had already arranged a student loan to pay for the reverse orthodontics. He knew what we didn't.

By the end of the Academic Year the paper, 'Voice loss in Performers: a pilot treatment programme to show the effect on the voice of correcting structural misalignment' had been accepted for publication and I gave my first presentation to a Voice Conference in Regensburg, taking my balls, stretch bands and balance boards to demonstrate the need for exercise if you were to take part in your own correction and build the muscles that would prevent regression. I was now able to load a peer reviewed paper linking voice and dental problems onto the website. I hoped singing teachers would now take the new information on the position of the tongue and the functional mechanics of the jaw more seriously.

But first there was an interview with the Head of the Music Department who was concerned at the number of singing students appearing wearing 'surgical equipment'. A consensus of other singing teachers in the department had ruled that resting the tongue back and up against the palate would close off the throat and was therefore not acceptable teaching of singing. I was dismissed. Well not exactly.... All of the students in my pilot study except my recovering voice were now at the end of their course. They merely put it that no new students would be sent to me from the University in the following academic year.

My recovering voice had two years to go and insisted on continuing his work with me. As double bass was his principal instrument this was accepted. Already the expansion of the dental arches, supported by sessions of chiropractic treatment and voice and body exercise to stabilize the changes to his balance and posture, had brought dramatic changes to his body. He was more athletic, all the pudginess had gone and as the roof of his mouth was widened and lengthened the voice that he had always known was there began to develop. Before his last University year he was auditioned by the Head of the Music Department, who accepted that his singing was now better than his bass playing and allowed him to change his solo instrument from double bass to voice.

Apart from the team that was managing his reverse orthodontics and me, everyone else was sceptical. How could he possibly think of becoming a singer with all that 'kit' in his mouth? But new techniques that used very light wire appliances had been developed and in his final student recital he sang easily and well with these Applied Light Function (ALFs) on upper and lower teeth. He was, however, penalised for wearing them in a recital that was also part of his final examination.

It took another three years to build the confidence destroyed when his voice disappeared apparently for no reason, but from the moment he had made the decision to reverse the orthodontics he had been assisting his own treatment, responsible for changing muscles with exercise, shifting his tongue into the roof of his mouth as it widened and making it his business to understand everything that happened to him. From the moment he made his own informed choices he was building his own confidence and the results say it all

Premolars removed

Premolars replaced

The website was now attracting enquiries from people with voice problems but there were no professional singers amongst them. The voice problems fell roughly into two groups. There was voice loss when using the voice in speech. These were mostly school teachers, who had been trained in all aspects of teaching except the most important – how to use the voice. Most did not sing so I designed a course that would give them the whole voice, supported by exercise. None had ever done any professional maintenance before.

By far the largest group were those who had read an article on the website describing what a terrible blow it had been for me to lose my singing and how it affected every facet of my life. None of these people were musicians and none had any particular vocal aspirations beyond the plea "If only I could sing".

The same story was repeated over and over. Someone; usually a school music teacher, but sometimes a parent, a sibling or just one's peers, had cut them off from singing by telling them when they were small and vulnerable, they couldn't sing. The test for the school choir and failure to be accepted for it was often a pivotal moment when they ceased to have music in their lives and it seemed that being tested for a choir could happen as early as seven or eight. I was angry to think that selection should occur so early. I had experienced such a wonderful voice development as a child with singing being fun and often to accompany dancing round the kitchen. Everyone sang in my primary school, every morning and last thing on Friday afternoons. I only encountered a choir in secondary school and even then there wasn't just *one* choir. Several of the teachers ran their own and there was healthy competition between that run by the senior master for Christmas, which was lots of noise but not much musical accuracy, and the Speech Day choir, all accuracy but not much 'Hwyl' (This is an untranslatable Welsh word; the nearest but still inadequate word in English is 'passion').

If you don't think you can sing because at six or seven you tried and failed you might well assume that you were not 'musical' Would you then buy your son an expensive flute on the evidence that he could not even make the choir? I needed to know more about this so next time I went to see my daughter, who still lives in the community where she went to school I chatted to some of her now grown up school friends about their own school singing.

Three middle schools fed into the local High School, where music was high on the agenda. One of the Middle schools had a singing specialist music teacher on the staff and this school provided the High School with the majority of the children who both sang and played instruments. In lunch times and after school instrumental teachers came in to give lessons, run a school orchestra and a wind band. There was now a thriving adult 'Big Band' jazz band that played all over the county for dances and functions. This band had developed from those school beginnings.

The Head of Music in the High School was also a singer but she did not have the inclusive policy of the teacher in the Middle School. Singing depended on selection for the choir and further selection within the choir for a special madrigal group of sixteen singers. Musical standards and no doubt numbers were maintained by including staff who sang. The madrigal group was in the main choir so taking out the staff the choir would be at most about forty strong.

There is no more daily school assembly at which everyone sings a hymn and regardless of the ethical arguments for and against, at least everyone then sings every day. Why not mass singing of a song every morning? Those whose singing had been axed by discouragement and selection could begin again in the noise that drowned their own voice every morning. Instead, when music becomes an option on the timetable, only those in the choir will leave school having singing in their lives. In this case forty out of a possible 2,000. From this particular school the 'Big Band,' thrives in the community and has a huge following but choirs in the area struggle to recruit members and audiences.

Even more interesting was the fact that all of my daughter's friends hated the music teacher because "she only spoke to you if you were in the choir". I asked what other teacher they hated and they looked puzzled. What on earth had prompted such a vitriolic reaction to the music teacher who taught the singing? Music has power and gives power to those who share it. Every religion, every ruler has always known that. We should all share in that musical power and what easier way than singing when we can all sing? People who have singing taken away from them are not just deprived of music. They are also deprived of personal power and we all resent that.

I was now speaking about the links between the voice and the development of the dentition at major International Orthodontic Conferences where having the tongue in the floor of the mouth was recognised as the onset of many orthodontic problems, the most severe of which was 'Tongue Thrust' that interfered with speech and breathing . My website contained information on the importance of tongue position, nose breathing, posture and regular structural and dental checks for anyone expecting to earn their living from their voice. Surely there must be singers out there who needed this information; after all I had encountered four by teaching just ten singing students at the University. But no singers came to see me, none enquired about references for my information. Perhaps the singers who were selected for a Specialist Music Colleges had no problems, had only to develop their vocal talents throughout the three or four years offered to them and step out into the world of auditions for places in Opera, Music Theatre, Professional Choirs or Concerts. From my own experience I knew that at least a few must fall by the way, as I had. I would have given my eye teeth to have been able to read my own website when I was nineteen so where were the few that had the problems? Why did they not turn up on my doorstep, or at least email some questions?

I thought back to my senior school and how much singing was included for everyone. Take out the choirs, which demanded that you go to practice in your own time, and what was left for *everybody* to do? The mass singing that ended all special days, like end of term, Battle of Britain, Saint David's Day and any other excuse for complete school assembly. Although all of these had special songs we all sang, like the Welsh National Anthem, Jerusalem or Bread of Heaven in Welsh, it was not considered enough to trot these out after a couple of practices the day before. We had to have regular school singing practices, for which we had a repertoire of songs for mass singing. This is a copy used in my own school for mass singing (and obviously lifted when I left). This must have been a popular thing to do by the number of titles listed from only one publisher.

CRAMER'S LIBRARY of UNISON and PART-SONGS

by Modern Composers

edited by

MARTIN SHAW

OLD NOTATION AND TONIC SOL-FA COMBINED

No. 9.

CARGOES

UNISON SONG

Words by JOHN MASEFIELD — Music by MARTIN SHAW

Suitable for

UNISON MASS-SINGING

9.	Cargoes	*Martin Shaw*
12.	Pilgrim Song	*Herbert Popple*
20.	Glad Hearts Adventuring	*Martin Shaw*
24.	The Moon is Up	*Norman O'Neill*
26.	Pioneers	*Martin Shaw*
41.	The West Country	*Norman O'Neill*
45.	Service	*Martin Shaw*
46.	Gather up your litter	*Martin Shaw*
51.	Perseverance	*Walter Adrian*
57.	Freedom	*M. Stewart Baxter*
59.	The Song of the Music Makers	*Martin Shaw*
66.	Song of the Lads of Devon	*Geoffrey Shaw*
68.	O Land of Britain	*Martin Shaw*
69.	Working Together	*Martin Shaw*
82.	Sea Shanty	*Martin Shaw*
84.	The Forward Road	*Herbert Popple*
86.	Ring out ye Crystal Spheres	*Geoffrey Shaw*
100.	Fight the Good Fight	*Geoffrey Shaw*
107.	The Builders	*Martin Shaw*
109.	The Breastplate	*William Every*
111.	The Invaders	*Colin Ross*
133.	A Chant for England	*Martin Shaw*
181.	Big Steamers	*Edward German*
196.	Drake's Drum	*Martin Shaw*

MASS-SINGING
(Continued)

197.	I Love all Beauteous Things (descant optional)	*Christopher Le Fleming*
198.	The Blossom	*Felix White*
203.	The Animal's Carol	*Thomas F. Dunhill*
206.	White and Silver	*Arthur Baynon*
208.	The Lark	*Arthur J. Pritchard*
216.	Sword of Youth	*Donald Ford*
222.	The Happy Heart	*Donald Ford*
223.	The Storke	*Dorothy Martin*
224.	The Whirl of Wheels	*Noel Cox*
231.	We thank Thee Lord	*Arthur J. Pritchard*
232.	The Promise	*Donald Ford*
238.	Unseen Comradeship	*Christopher Le Fleming*
240.	Coronation Song	*Martin Shaw*
246.	Buttercups	*Ivy Frances Klein*

COMPLETE LIST ON APPLICATION

J. B. CRAMER & CO., LTD.
99, ST. MARTIN'S LANE, LONDON, W.C.2.

Wellington, N.Z.: CHAS. BEGG & CO. LTD.
Winnipeg: WESTERN MUSIC CO.
Sydney: W. H. PALING & CO. LTD.

MADE IN ENGLAND

Chapter 17: The Training Track

The young man who had been given his premolars back was now a professional singer meeting other young working singers, most of whom had spent at least three years at a specialist Music College. He began to realize that many of them felt very insecure and nervous at auditions and performances, hoping that 'everything would go well today' but if it did, unsure why it did. Many admitted to having minor problems with their voices that they did not expect to solve because no one seemed to have the answer. So why weren't they beating on the doors of the Music Colleges demanding to know why their voice did not do what they knew it could? Why did singers assume immediate personal responsibility for not being a success? Did no one ever question whether they had been badly taught and complain about it? Apparently not. Not when I was training forty years ago and not now. This may be the reason why little had changed in the training of singers in forty years, or even maybe forty years before that.

In not being as good as that other person who had just got the job, walked the audition, gained the place in the opera school you have failed to please.

That desire to please, how well I knew it. It was there every time I opened my mouth to sing. The desire to please, to hide problems and feel that problems had to be your own inadequacy was definitely something to do with singing lessons. Perhaps I was too young when I went to Music College and over awed by being accepted for such a prestigious training? I know that there was an excitement akin to nerves about going into my singing lesson. I wanted praise for what I did and if I felt I had not sung as well as I could, or failed to execute every exercise so that my teacher smiled approval I would come away determined to practice and make up deficiencies. Deficiencies? How could I have developed the idea that every lesson was some kind of performance? When I had been selected as someone worthy of a place to study at one of the top Music Colleges why was I so nervous about being worthy so much of the time? When I felt I had not done as well a I might I would go into the refectory and someone would say. "Are you OK? Had a bad lesson? I had one last week. Forget it. It'll be better next time" It was a familiar camaraderie among singers. What had it to do with learning, questioning paradigms, moving on?

How different when I wanted to learn from the .clinicians. I had quite a different attitude. I argued, questioned, needed to understand and be satisfied that I did. When I had fastened onto something, like a ferret, I did not let go until the unanswered question was fully explained...with references! Then I went and checked it out for myself.

According to the internet there are twelve Premier Music Colleges in the United Kingdom offering training for professional singing. Many more offer Performance training that includes singing. If each one of the Premier Colleges takes only ten singers a year to train that is 120 students. In five years that is 600 hopeful singers. Where do all these singers go? Where do they all earn their living? The increased cost of mounting live performances, the increase in recorded sales, plus the ability of technology to add manufactured voices in recordings has reduced the marketplace for everyone except the most versatile singer/musicians.

But are the singers from this specialist training likely to be versatile? According to the websites of these colleges the bulk of the vocal material studied in individual lessons is early Italian song of the 17th and 18th centuries, German lieder of the 19th Century, French art songs and 20th century English song. There are postgraduate Opera courses if you show particular flair, but the numbers remain excessive for this market. One college of the twelve states that the singing teaching will be 'classical' and for that reason no time will be spent on Jazz, pop, or other vocal singing styles. A browse down the list of singing teachers confirms this. Most belong or have belonged to the world of classical song, oratorio and opera; the recital, the concert and the song cycle. Music Theatre is a growing postgraduate training but the list of teachers providing the fundamental three year training includes very few who have been particularly successful or experienced in this field.

Are 120 singers a year going to give a Wigmore Hall recital and when they have, where will their next one be? The nearest most will get to a recital is the programme they will sing for their diploma in singing at the end of their course. Knowing this they are likely to opt for a teaching rather than performance diploma as this will give them something to fall back on if they do not 'make it'. I first began teaching singing because I could teach in the evening when my small children were in bed and bring in a second income. I sent for a syllabus to tell me where to begin. It did not tell me how to begin if the person I were teaching did not already sing, but only to test what he or she could already do. No one came who did not sing until I wrote my website thirty years later.

The newly qualified singing teachers who opt out of performance or who are still auditioning but as yet have no work are encouraged to perpetuate the system they have been trained on by teaching to the examination systems set by the Colleges. Eight possible grade examinations progress you year by year, singing Italian, German and English songs, maybe a study and plenty of scales and exercises. The later grades pay lip service to popular music by including Gershwin, Cole Porter or songs of a similar 'swing' style, but it is unlikely that your examiners have ever performed such music themselves. It is possible to arrive at the last grade without ever having sung to anyone but your teacher and an examiner. How can you learn to 'play' the voice when there is only testing for correctness when you sing?

The teachers from the Colleges will examine the entrants to the Grade examinations at local Centres, looking for the methods and techniques that they taught the teachers. This completes the closed loop of professional singing training and it is this closed loop that produces most of the hopeful entrants for the twelve Specialist Music Colleges. You step into this closed loop at fourteen or fifteen when you select your singing teacher from the list of members of the Incorporated Society of Musicians, the ICM, the union of classical teachers and performers. It is likely that your teacher will aim for you to go to his or her old College and those who come nearest to supplying the qualities established through years of refining the system are the most likely to get in.

There you can have more of the judgement, this time surrounded by international competition for very few professional places. For three or maybe four years you will be in a one to one learning situation with one specialist teacher of your instrument. You would have to make a very strong case to change that teacher, who has power over your singing, where you go with it, your joy of music and consequently your confidence. Within the closed unit that is the department of singing you need to give a great performance every time you open your mouth and impress in lessons and in classes. That way you may make sufficient impression over the three years to get a foot on the working ladder before you leave. But this does not allow for experimenting with the development of your voice, you do not have time for problems and there are other singers to replace you in performance if you do.

Of course there are those who escape this loop because they are exceptional. They are the names we see on the CDs and in the opera houses and the Music Theatres. They do get to sing at the Wigmore and Queen Elizabeth Halls and in the Proms. But there are few of them compared to the numbers of 'trained' singers we are turning out year by year with very little chance of earning a living except by private teaching – yet still are not trained in voice mechanics and functional anatomy to use in their teaching because the loop perpetuates the belief system that performance is the only worthwhile career to be training for. Who needs to be an expert in voice problems, singers are not supposed to have them.

What happens before you are ready to have singing lessons?

Once you go into school at four or five years old the voice will be for ever separated for you into speech and singing.

"That is the room with the piano and that is where you go to sing"

You have a special person –

"This is Mrs Evans, she will take you for singing on Thursday mornings"

– but she may not sing, she may just have audio equipment and backing tracks of children's songs, perpetuating the idea that you only sing when you are little and then grow out of it. It follows in most people's logic that singing and speech operate differently and even are actually two different voices. Thus people who can keep an audience in thrall with an on the fly performance in speech, like some teachers, politicians and actors often claim they cannot sing. Those who avoid swimming are probably not very familiar with having fun in the water.. It's a question of familiarity and exercise with lots encouragement and enjoyment thrown in.

So you sing only in the music room, which encourages the belief, certainly throughout the United Kingdom, that only musical people sing. By the time a child is ten singing has become accepted as a specialist musical activity – see the previous chapter - and lessons are needed to teach you how to do it *properly.* There is also quite a financial and educational advantage in being able to offer singing to gain entry to private education. Choir schools offer scholarship places to children who sing well and have music skills like sight reading. For a boy with a fine treble voice the prospect of going free to a very good school more than compensates for the extra hours added to every day for practices and services in the Cathedral. This is now also open to girls.

Over control and over selection prevents many people from seeking lessons. There is a real fear in the general population that a singing teacher will make you sound unnatural and stiff and with good cause, because many trained singers with all play and joy removed from their voices do sound like that. On the other hand a nightmare maverick bunch exists to 'turn you into a pop idol' or make a demo for you to lead to your first recording contract – at a price. Outside the closed loop of the examination track anyone who plays a keyboard or even has relevant backing tracks can teach singing. We have already discovered how vulnerable are people who want to sing. There are hundreds of boxed CD singing methods to choose from and absolutely no means of preventing the worst and most damaging. In between these two extremes are courses that will get you singing and expressing yourself for a day or a weekend, but after that how do you continue?

I look back with gratitude and delight at my own musical development and the opportunities there were for singing to people. The Sunday night concerts at the seaside where I sang the popular music of the day were my training ground for performance. No matter that the elephants farted in the background, it was all part of the education. My desire to sing and to please was fuelled by those audiences who had come to enjoy themselves and hear this young girl sing, no microphone, no reverb, no mixing desk, just me doing what I could do. Singing was fun and my voice developed like a young tree, out in all kinds of weathers, so it grew strong and lovely. When I came to take exams I already knew how to sing to people and how to present the story that is in all music. I learned the songs accurately but sang them totally from the heart, with no fear. Fear came only with the atmosphere of judgement in the Music College. Fear became terror with the realisation that those teaching me did not know anything about the voice, only about the music. That was a huge shock. It was now another shock to discover that nothing had changed in the years between.

If in-depth study of music has been turning out at least a hundred and twenty singers a year and has been doing so since I went to Music College forty years ago you would think that some of it should have rubbed off on this island population if it were at all enjoyable and we would by now be a singing nation. More local concerts would be happening with more performers and more audiences. Yet we remain a nation that cannot sing and are terrified of the thought of getting up in front of people and singing. When I asked a woman in a workshop, who was doing rather well and gathering confidence every minute whether she would be prepared to sing on her own, she said.

"I would rather take my clothes off. It would be less embarrassing and less terrifying."

I suspect many people feel the same. A good Karaoke operator can make anyone feel wonderful and powerful, especially where the decision to 'go for it' is well oiled by alcohol. It demonstrates the need people have to feel wonderful and there should be lots of singing teachers who can get that for them from a standing start *and* create opportunities in the community to sing that are not judgemental. It is a basic human need to sing, so the TV singing shows may have to audition and reject 6,000 people from just one area, and the marketers of dreams have the non singing population by the short and curlies. All because the qualified singing teachers are very selective about who would benefit from lessons and most of the population does not qualify.

Is it this 'them and us' that is the real divide between classical and popular singing? Does the majority of the population hate classical singing for the same reasons that most of the young people in my daughter's High School hated the woman who ran the singing in the music department; because there is a terrible exclusion that is deeply felt. So people will save for an expensive ticket to hear Elton John but they will not stir out of their houses to hear the local girl making good in the concert at the Town Hall. On the one hand Elton John is one of them, probably also a reject in terms of singing lessons as they are understood whereas the local girl who went to Music college to learn to sing was probably selected for that because she was not like most of us, she was 'musical'. Rejection is very powerful.

My website was five years old before the first professionally trained singer came to see what could be done for her because her voice was failing. She was the first of many who met someone in a pub and was told 'there are answers to your problems'.

She was reluctant to tell her teacher that she was worried about her singing and afraid that her agent would find out. There was a real fear of anyone getting to know, which probably explained why she had been given my name in a pub. I was a name whispered and a telephone number scribbled down. Someone outside London who could get you a 'fix'. Work may be in short supply but this is ridiculous. Who can ever go through a professional life in any field without hitting a problem? Are performers of so little value, or of so little quality that they can be disposed of if their jaw hurts?

Her jaw was being driven back into the joint by the way she was opening her mouth. She was singing with a flat tongue and when told to 'drop the jaw' this singer did it in quite the wrong way. Her teacher apparently did not know the difference. The exercises and ascending scales that encouraged effort, the lack of any relevant body exercise, her lack of information on what she was doing and the fear factor of not being good enough all combined to drive the jaw back so that her singing had first became uncomfortable and then lost its quality. The singing lessons had begun at fifteen and she was now twenty six. Because of the recycling of information in the teaching 'loop' and no up to date information able to break in, this singer had driven the jaw back throughout her training. The voice needed to be most reliable now she had to earn her living but the accommodation she had developed for dealing with the struggling muscles was coming to an end and she was in pain.

A trickle of musicians now began to appear. A horn player came after I gave a talk on the jaw at his College and admitted that he had been in *slight* pain for at least a year and it had suddenly become worse just when he was having auditions for major orchestras and having to play more hours – surprise, surprise. When I asked what his teacher thought about this he admitted he had never told his teacher because his teacher often gave him paid work to deputize for him in concerts. "He probably won't give me work if he knows I have a problem"

The singers who arrived were equally afraid of upsetting teachers who were 'so nice' and 'has done so much for me ', but these were people whose music was slipping away from them. Imagine a competing athlete discovering that the physiotherapist was upsetting muscle balance in his legs and that was why he was losing races. Is it likely that he would not do anything about it in case he upset the physiotherapist? The power that someone can have over a singer with even one shred of personal doubt is incredible. But I had found that out already for myself the hard way.

These musicians had read papers and articles from my website and already made the decision to change whatever had to be changed to sing and play well. Their lives were already committed to professional music and for the first time I detected a motivation that would not opt for teaching as the easy way out. They all acknowledged that teaching was a step further and not a step back. For each singer a team was set up. An orthodontist, to expand the maxilla and encourage the jaw to move down and forward; a cranial chiropractor or cranial osteopath, who supported the dental work and checked for structural misalignment, often finding the remains of birth trauma in the behaviour of the cranial bones; I re-programmed the articulation of words and changed the position of the tongue. This had to be done in every case because every singer had been taught that the tongue should lie in the floor of the mouth with the tip against the bottom teeth. Many had struggled to keep it there throughout their training and were now about to pass on that information to the next generation of young singers.

All have improved, jaws are functionally sound and all the singers that came and were corrected are now back earning their living- except one, who had his premolars removed. He will teach for two years to earn the money to have expansion of the arches and the teeth replaced because his tongue will not fit into the present small roof of his mouth. It is important to note that none of this money would have needed to be spent if there were a policy in place to check young performers between ten and fifteen years old structurally and dentally; if early orthodontics prevented extractions and jaw muscle function in relation to singing and playing wind instruments was explained. Currently there is nothing in place to protect the young musician from the later development of physical problems.

Another panic area emerged from working with these singers. There is apparently no point in doing anything about your problems if you are pushing thirty. Anyone who has not made it in the UK as a singer by thirty will not make it at all because you are then too old. Better go into teaching after that. There is only a lower age limit of seventeen on training to be a singer, according to the Colleges' website and no upper age limit is disclosed in any of the Music College entrance application. However there *are* upper limits, usually of twenty five, imposed on all competitions and scholarships I have ever seen advertised. If we look at performance of speech, to discourage actors after the age of thirty would lose us most of the best. Maybe it goes back to early school when we chattered all day in every classroom and then went to sing only on Thursdays in the music room. Singing just never got strong enough, not in our bodies and not in our lives. What are we doing to the function of singing that it is expected to fail early in the thirties? Or is it that singing *is* failing in the thirties in so many cases that we have to pretend that is natural for it to do so?

One Music Centre that specializes in short courses runs a two day 'singing for the over sixties' I wonder if it is like keep fit for the over sixties with concessions for age and inflexibility.

Move over Carreras, Domingo, Dolly Parton and all the rest!

Chapter 18: A Fresh Start

The other ducks were pecking and harassing her
While she sat tight upon the grass
She fixed me with an eye, impenetrable, black
And dared me harm her. So I gently tucked her
Underneath my arm to put her in a straw-filled box.
She laid her head down in the grass, Neck limp , eye dull.
I'd seen it often, first the pecking, then submission
And then a quiet death.
"Is that OK? Now when you die
At least you'll die in comfort".
She looked at me, we knew each other well.
I'd watched her chase the other ducks
To swim and preen...
"Poor duck" I said and stroked her,

I crouched beside her miserably and wished I could do more.
Her black eye met my own; she tipped her beak, smiled,
Shook herself and laid a perfect egg.

Maybe the challenge that no one could begin a career in performance after thirty was too much to ignore. Maybe I had spent too many years giving others the chance to sing and then going to listen to them. Whatever it was that caused it did not really matter. What mattered was that suddenly I wanted to please people again with my singing as I had so many years ago. Wait a minute, after thirty is a challenge, after forty is a midlife crisis. You are now 68. So now I have nothing to lose and it's what I want to do. I don't have to burn cities with my singing, or even CDs. I don't have to be famous, but my singing is what I have been working for all this time. Most of my life has been about recovering my singing. So now

I've recovered it, why don't I do it? I need to sing to people because it makes me feel wonderful and that is something everyone needs at all times of their lives.

This is what I must do. First make time to work on it, do the work you have made everyone else do. Then find a pianist to play for you who will work for music at its best yet not be judgemental while you ease the voice back into speed and agility. Choose your repertoire carefully. Put aside all the songs about young girl's dreams, first love and naivety. You will never sing them convincingly again. But songs of life experience that eluded you when you were young will be totally changed for you now. You will understand the songs of loss, birth and death as you never did before and sing them with the balance and stability that you have gained.

Because I now sang using my whole body I found that my voice expressed what I felt without the cosmetic planning of what to do with each musical phrase. I was no longer telling my voice how to sing, I was maintaining stability in myself and allowing the voice to sing itself. This singing was new and much more exciting. I was not learning songs with any thought of performance this time, but searching for the story, to understand it and learn why the composer did this or that with the words. I began to appreciate the way composers used words and that good songs were across the musical spectrum. I had always sung all kinds of music but the divide between classical and 'other' had always been there in my head because it had been such a divide for those who had originally trained me. Instead of choosing those songs that would show my voice off to best advantage I now chose a programme by deciding what kind of people would be in the audience and what they would want to hear.

I had previously always chosen a song for its music. First played the tune, noted its rise and fall and imagined how my voice would sound at this pitch or sustaining this sound for this long. My voice had always came first; I noted which bits of the music I would do well, aim to shine on this top note. I was good at doing this particular musical acrobatic but I would have to work hard on this one and plan my approach road carefully. When I had finally got to grips with how my voice would perform the music I pegged the words onto the tune like so many clothes on a line. This is how I was taught and I had never thought of it any other way.

Now I deliberately changed the way I chose music to sing. I searched through my old repertoire for words that grabbed me, words I felt I understood and might have written myself only not quite as well. Then I played the song on the piano and read the words to the tune, observing the colours in the harmony that pointed to the emotional line within the musical line. I had never learned songs like this before. It felt like learning from the bottom up and it was a revelation. I knew so much about singing now and yet I felt I was learning all over again from an entirely different perspective; from what drove the composer of the song to write it in the first place. My voice seemed secondary to what I had to say, but as if it had finally found its place, it behaved better.

This method of selection juxtaposed music of apparently opposing musical styles. People in every walk of life and in all religions and periods of history have faced the same fundamental struggles and satisfactions and where this pop song added yet more weight to the same thoughts in Rachmaninov or Sondheim or Mozart, why not bring them into the same musical conversation?

While I was enjoying the prospect of a whole new life of singing I made the mistake of mentioning to a colleague that I wanted to sing again and may try to put a concert together; that I was making time to practice and to work with a pianist. I know now it is possible to sing well, even in your late sixties. You just have to be mentally alert, well balanced and physically flexible, have good free function of the jaw and the desire to make music to give you confidence, Of course you may not have the muscle power to compete with the young but I was already seeing another way of being musically interesting. When I voiced this intention to my colleague the negative comments I received put me back weeks. No use telling myself that I was expressing the joy I felt at being alive and that I knew my voice would sing well again if I gave it some time and TLC.

Apparently nobody got up and sang at my age, well not seriously, maybe for a bit of fun, or at Christmas 'when you'd had a few' and it was pretty obvious that the aim was to save me and my potential audience from acute embarrassment. The doubt that I had anything to offer turned immediately into self doubt and I avoided singing my new and exciting repertoire for about a month, cancelling my first practice with my pianist with some lame excuse, like too busy.

Meanwhile I watched the London Marathon on the TV and saw veteran marathon runners of fifty, sixty, seventy and even older taking part in the same race as everyone else. I went back to my colleague.

"I've decided to take up running. I watched the London Marathon and I think if I train all this year I might have a go at it next year. Of course it is years since I ran. I played hockey really well, played for a league team, but I don't know.... Maybe I'm getting old and it's just one of my fantasies, you know, hanging on to your dreams. "

"Dreams are really important. Lots of people as old as you take up sports. I play badminton. I'm not very good but I so enjoy it. You run, and don't be put off by people who say "what do you want to do that for?"

I didn't bother to remind him of our conversation about my singing, but went back to my practicing and pinned this on the wall next to the piano.

"But why, you ask me, should this tale be told
To men grown old, or who are growing old?
It is too late! Ah, nothing is too late
Till the tired heart shall cease to palpitate.
Cato learned Greek at eighty; Sophocles
Wrote his grand Oedipus, and Simonides
Bore off the prize of verse from his compeers,
When each had numbered more than fourscore years,
And Theophrastus, at fourscore and ten,
Had but begun his Characters of Men.
Chaucer, at Woodstock with the nightingales,
At sixty wrote the Canterbury Tales;
Goethe at Weimar, toiling to the last,
Completed Faust when eighty years were past.
These are indeed exceptions; but they show
How far the gulf-stream of our youth may flow
Into the arctic regions of our lives.
Where little else than life itself survives.

What then? Shall we sit idly down and say
The night hath come; it is no longer day?
The night hath not yet come; we are not quite
Cut off from labour by the failing light;
Something remains for us to do or dare;
Even the oldest tree some fruit may bear;
Not Oedipus Coloneus, or Greek Ode,
Or tales of pilgrims that one morning rode
Out of the gateway of the Tabard inn,
But other something, would we but begin;
For age is opportunity no less
Than youth itself, though in another dress,
And as the evening twilight fades away
The sky is filled with stars, invisible by day.

Extract from Morituri Salutamus (1875)
Written and delivered by Longfellow at the 50th anniversary of the class of 1825 in Bowdoin College

Before I could rearrange the appointment with my accompanist I was summoned to the local hospital for my annual breast cancer check. I was first diagnosed with breast cancer in 1998, while still searching for an answer to the hip problem. It did not come as a surprise. I had endured seven years of attempts to correct my bite, the torsion in my skull and the 'falling over'. Before that my life had been one of continual stress and distress. My limited information on chronic illness suggested that it often occurred as a result of severe trauma. I had come into the world with trauma and had been trying to discover the answer to it ever since. I had been fighting the Dental Distress Syndrome all my life so my reaction was that this was to be expected. By 1998 my teeth had finally been crowned. The seven years of orthodontics were completed on the Friday before I was given a lumpectomy on the Monday. The consultant surgeon's message was

"You are lucky. This is an early detection. After your operation you will be able to go away and get on with your life"

He looked most surprised when I tried to explain that I felt my breast cancer to be expected and probably the result of a life of dental distress plus the compensations I had added to my life to cope with that. I agreed with him that I was finally at a point where I could get on with my life as all that stress had been removed.

I did feel incredibly lucky, that the devil was finally out of my life and the angel definitely watching over me again. It was another message to return to singing, as if everything was falling into place.

A month later I was given radiotherapy for thirty days and advised to attend counselling during this treatment 'to help you to cope'. The last thing I wanted to do was talk about my cancer. I wanted to talk about what I could do now that I had been lucky enough to have my life saved by early detection. I was advised not to drive, but accepting the lift to my radiotherapy would keep me in the hospital for most of the day. I booked the earliest radiotherapy appointment possible, 8.30 am, and went on my bike. By 9.30 am I was back home and although I was tired I felt I was in charge of myself. After a sleep I tried to play the piano but lymph glands under my arm had been removed along with muscle tissue and my left hand was reluctant. It was to take me two years to rebuild the muscle and recover my piano playing. The lymph glands removed were completely clear of any cancer cells. I was angry that yet another important working bit of me had been unnecessarily removed but consoled myself that this was not like the dental extractions. This time I could have died and now I could…what did he say?

"Go and get on with my life"

I told only closest friends about the breast cancer because I soon discovered that there was a terror of the 'big C' and in the public imagination you were indeed destined to die. I didn't need this negative stuff, it was not helpful. I was given the drug Tamoxifen, told it was standard and I must take it for five years. After a month my voice had become baritone and my vision blurred. I also put on lots of weight. I felt exhausted and generally miserable so I stopped taking the drug. None of this went down very well with the cancer unit looking after me and I felt very guilty that I was not doing as I was told when these people had saved my life. However, I had by this time found Mr McMinn of the Hip

Resurfacing Project and the prospect of removing the last of my pain was so compelling I was no longer focused on the breast cancer.

Two years later, having finally dealt with the two areas that had been having the wrong conversations all of my life, my hips and my jaw, and got them to agree to work together, cancer was diagnosed in the other breast and I was summoned for another consultation.

The consultant surgeon was very positive. "We need to do the same operation on the other side. It is quite common for this to happen. We removed the cancer entirely from one breast, we just need to remove it from the other. I will take some lymphatic tissue from the right arm to check for any spread but everything proceeded very well last time, you are very healthy and I do not anticipate any problems. We will give you radiotherapy and then you can go and get on with your life"

I was now balanced on two feet thanks to Mr McMinn. I had recovered my under arm muscles with exercise, my body felt comfortable and I was back to singing and playing the piano. I was not *quite* so easy to convince that I would be able to get on with my life after this operation. I had heard that before. I agreed to a lumpectomy but no loss of lymphatic tissue. This would save the muscles that traversed my armpit. I needed those for breathing, playing the piano, singing and so much else. It had been such hard work to recover them and they had been damaged for no good reason that I could see.

I tried to discuss this to the surgeon without success. He did not want a lesson in anatomy from one of his patients. That was his field. But the patient's charter did not allow him to have the ultimate word so this time there was one day in hospital, no removal of lymphatic tissue, no radiotherapy and no drugs. I had the distinct feeling that the 'N' for No that appeared in all the little tick boxes for auxiliary procedures also represented 'Nuisance'.

When the summons came again in 2004 after the annual mammogram I was shocked. So much had been sorted out and I was so much more confident, positive and alive. I was working with singers and making plans to sing myself. I had learnt a new Beethoven Sonata, the first new piano music I had learned in years. Even my brain was working more efficiently. I was writing articles and giving really good presentations on the team work of interdisciplinary correction. I had free time for my singing, for playing the piano and for expanding the network of clinicians who could work with voice problems.

My hospital record was not good. As well as a history of breast cancer I had a history of questioning treatment protocol. I was about to question it some more. I refused a biopsy on the grounds that the damage to tissue may spread the problem and called a halt to the planning of yet another operation 'as soon as possible so that the cancer is contained'. This time I did not go into automatic fear mode at this prospect. I felt much too alive.

"I want to go away and think this through. This is the third time I have been diagnosed with breast cancer. Why am I getting cancer? I am taking care of myself now and I have to understand what I am doing to repeatedly fall chronically ill. You want me to go through another traumatic surgical procedure, but I feel as if I am on a surgical treadmill. The mammogram has 'hot spots' but there could be other reasons for that. You say that because it is only two years since my last operation the tumour is tiny, so why can't we see what it does if we leave it alone for a bit? Maybe the growth rate is so slow that I'd be dead and buried naturally before it became a problem. Maybe it will even go away. Why are we panicking about this and arranging an operation as soon as possible? I am not afraid to leave it for a couple of months to see what it does so why should you be?"

The consultant surgeon reminded me patiently that the unit was not responsible for me if I refused all advice. I had a history of breast cancer. If I wouldn't have a biopsy there was no way of knowing whether the shadows were malignant and if they were I may well die. As I sat listening to him I wondered if the fact that he was a surgeon meant that all he could do with my cancer was cut it out. If the head of the Breast cancer Unit who made the rules were a surgeon, what other way could there ever be? Why did I feel like a naughty child because thoughts like these occurred? Because I suddenly saw myself as another justification for his getting up in the morning? Because I was trying to find an alternate route *yet again*?

I was beginning to see parallels with so many of the times I had needed help. The need for help reduced my personal power and the consultant told me what would happen, how I would be helped and I dumbly allowed it. Nothing was discussed. The very word 'consultant' indicated that I would only listen but not speak, like the word 'God' often prevents further questioning. There had been so many times when I had felt out of control of my own life ; the laryngologist who burned out the top of my nose; the doctor who wanted to give me something to 'calm me down' when I was desperate about the state of my voice; the orthodontist, who removed four excellent teeth without explanation; the hip surgeon, who expected me to return 'when the pain was great enough'. In all of these situations I had felt put down and powerless, except in the case of the hip. There I had found my own solution, but it had still cost me. I should have gone back and demanded that the NHS pay for the operation I had found that was better for me. Considering these experiences made me feel that I was changing and that I was possibly more stable. This time I was going to make sure that what happened next was best for me.

I was given three months to consider my position and at the end of it I decided that the cancer unit was trying to save my life and I was not being appreciative. I must somehow try to set up a dialogue instead of just appearing to refuse all advice. I contacted the Bristol Cancer Centre and discovered the importance of having a very positive purpose to live for and making time to express yourself and your emotions through music, painting or similar spiritual nutrition. I also discovered that several cancer units, led by the one in Cardiff, were learning a new procedure, where a central lymph node was examined without the need for the underarm surgery. Attitude appeared to be crucial. You must have something important to live for and keep negativity well at bay. When I returned for my next appointment the biopsy had been cancelled. Instead I was to have a full MRI scan and an appointment made to discuss the results and the next move. I was given no opportunity to tell anyone what I had discovered and could not help thinking I was being blinded by science.

When I went home Chris was furious, but not with me. His scientific training was replacing the fear for me and he was analyzing the treatment I had had so far.

"This is the third time they have repeated the same procedure. Einstein's definition of madness was doing the same thing over and over again and expecting to access change. Someone must have tried alternative treatments. Why haven't you been given any other information, if only to prove the case for surgery?"

Where I had looked inside for strength to withstand what was the only treatment on offer he embarked upon a research project. Night after night he hunted the internet for websites that offered information on other treatments. Every surface in the office carried piles of paper clipped together with labels; DIET, HORMONES, FOOD ADDITIVES, SUPPLEMENTS. There was a regular delivery of new books to the front door. It became clear that there was a world of information out there that I had not been given. Either it was not known by the cancer unit, which I found difficult to believe considering how quickly and easily we had come by it, or maybe I was just given their 'one true way'. Once more I felt important decisions had been made about me and for me without recognition that I was responsible ultimately for myself. My, how I had changed, and what support I had for that change.

We took a two-week holiday and booked a cheap flight to Spain, taking a tent, all camping needs and the books. Holed up beside a little bay, with a small beach, a few fish restaurants and not many tourists we made breast cancer our entire world. When we learned the importance of diet from at least five different sources the trips to the Supermarket left out dairy products and pastries and piled on the fresh fish, fresh meat, fruit and vegetables. We could have chosen no better place than a

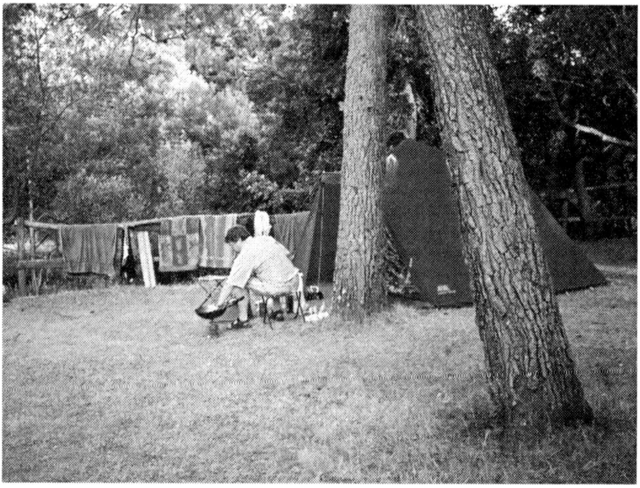

Mediterranean country to change our diet. My picture of this chronic illness changed and I lost my fear of it. I cried a lot and under the cool dark green pines, the shafts of sunlight breaking through, it felt a positive and cleansing thing to do.

On the last day we summed up what we had learned. I needed to have much more specific tests than I had ever been given to restore hormone balance and whether I was deficient in any important nutrients. We must change very simple habits to make big differences, like always eating breakfast, but the main thing we had both learned was that we all have the potential for cancer, I was not different. Something; an event, a set of internal or external circumstances, triggered these rogue cells and there were plenty of examples of this process being reversed and the cancer going away.

Back home there was notice of my operation. I wrote to the consultant surgeon explaining why I had decided to cancel it and requesting that I be monitored with scans every three months while I attempted to reverse the growth of the tumour and achieve remission. That I had to save my music and what we had discovered, including the titles of the books we had read. I was sent an appointment.

Chris came to my appointment this time. He had wanted to accompany me on all the previous occasions but I was afraid that he would find it upsetting and transfer that to me. When I was first diagnosed he behaved like everyone else and expected me to die. I felt that if he did not get involved with sitting in the waiting room with the women who looked so fearful and dejected we would both cope. I made sure he only saw what was positive, what was recovery and he was delighted to help with that. We didn't talk 'cancer' at home, but only what we could do and where we could go after it and that helped me more than all the counselling.

This appointment was not at the unit but at the main hospital. When we were called I was asked to take off all clothes above the waist and given a small cape that tied at the front so that the consultant could examine me. We then both sat, me on a bed, Chris on a chair, for twenty minutes, waiting. When the consultant arrived he was not the one I had written to or who had dealt with me so far. He was an Asian doctor, who lifted my cape and moved to examine me. When I expressed indignation that I was not meeting with the consultant I had written to he threw up his hands in apology and said there was no need for me to see *him.* He was gone before I could say that it was definitely not his race that caused my indignation and I was left agonizing over my blunder, both breasts exposed and swinging.

Sometime later the consultant I recognised and had written to appeared. By then I had had no clothes on my upper half for nearly an hour and I was cold and felt undignified. His nurse carried a fat folder which was shuffled to find my letter. It was there but he had not read it. He examined me and then we discussed the next move, he standing in his white coat with his two assistants, me still bare breasted. trying to have a one to one conversation about saving my life. It was pretty one sided. Surgery came down face up. All I could do was refuse it, disempowered but determined.

Back at home Chris was fit to be tied. He could not believe that anyone was subjected to that degree of complete humiliation. But then if you are never put in the situation where you need to make waves how do you know? If all the authority works for you why not use it to make life easy?

I booked an appointment with a doctor practicing holistic medicine who arranged saliva, blood and hair tests. These discovered I had an under functioning thyroid, I was deficient in a number of important minerals and I was producing oestrogen like there was no tomorrow. I was prescribed natural supplements and also began to select much more carefully what I rubbed on my skin and washed into my hair. I now felt neither brave nor stupid for cancelling my operation, just that I had weighed the evidence and come to the only possible decision on that evidence.

But I was in the computer as an unresolved cancer treatment. I was summoned for another consultation to discuss the MRI. Chris and I arrived for the appointment and I was called for my mammogram.

"I have an appointment to discuss the results of an MRI, not a mammogram."

The nurse's voice rang down the corridor and through the waiting room.

"Mrs Lewis has refused a mammogram"

To me. "Would you wait in the waiting room, we will call you shortly"

We were eventually summoned. The folder containing my history of cancer sat on the desk, fat and strapped up with a tape to prevent all of the collected data falling out. In the big chair was a large lady consultant surgeon and next to her was someone who may have been a breast cancer nurse. Chris and I sat on chairs on the periphery and waited in silence while the consultant examined the result of my MRI scan. Eventually she turned to me, looking at me hard.

"This has gone on long enough. I see evidence of at least one tumour in the right breast and activity here"

She pointed to the edge of the breast tissue towards my armpit.

"This activity should be dealt with as soon as possible"

I noticed that she was South African, pronouncing activity as *ecteeveetee*.

"My *edvice*" I couldn't stop noticing it now, "is that you should *hev* a full mastectomy of the right breast and removal of relevant lymphatic tissue to prevent the spread of *cencer* to other organs. After a month I recommend a course of radiotherapy to target specific tissue and chemo therapy to follow when appropriate"

Behind me there was a sharp intake of breath.

"Oh Christ" murmured Chris.

Everything in the room became suddenly very clear as though the sun had come out outside and shone in through the window. There had been another moment like this but for a moment it eluded me and then when I looked for the sun at the window I noticed the top window was open. I remembered going to shut the one in the bathroom when the children were little and I had fallen down the concrete steps and not hurt myself. That too had been a moment when I knew something had changed and I had to move on.

"I have played the piano since I was four. Music is not something I learned, it grew inside me, it *is* me. I know I will not be able to sing and play with so much muscle damage. If I lose my music I may as well lose my life so I have to find another way to beat this besides having surgery".

"I cannot believe you *cen* be so irresponsible. There is no other way. The *cencer* must be removed and quickly. I can book you in for surgery in two months. The nurse will give you details. I suggest that your way you will lose both your music and your life. This way at least you will *hev* your life".

The barricade was too high and too strong. The consultant surgeon had only one way of dealing with my problem but at least she had a way. I had no answer except for a gut feeling that I had not come so far fighting for my music to give in now.

I sat quiet, thinking and watching her waiting for me to comply. How comfortable it must be to be so sure that you are right, to be so secure on your own island of knowledge, evangelical and steeped in the one truth.

I thanked her and turned down her offer. I could now go and get on with my life.

I do not want to lose the trees, the sky, the rise of sun at morn.
So many all important things came to naught in three short weeks.
A culling of my life where it had been so full.
My head had given up, lost control, was fearful,
Only my heart and spirit knew just what to cherish, what to cast aside.
So now I watch the trees, the sky, the rise of sun, and sing
'I love my love and know that he loves me'.

Post Script

Music is an incredibly powerful force, no matter how you make it. Compelling and beautiful music demands that both the player and the instrument itself have qualities of symmetry, balance and coordination. The hammers in the piano are all the same weight and shape, the pads on the flute keys close the holes exactly and the wood of the violin is chosen for its resonance from hundreds of rejections. All the different parts of an instrument are carefully assembled to balance well when held for maximum facility of fingers, hands and arms, maybe even more of the body of the player. Keyboards are weighted precisely to suit the touch of this or that pianist or the music to be played. The art of making a quality musical instrument is as old as our species and as carefully and beautifully developed.

Technology has improved many of the processes by which precision parts can be made, so high quality musical instruments are available to more people. Whereas a hundred years ago a young musician was unlikely to be able to afford a top quality instrument unless there was a wealthy family or patron to draw on, young musicians still training and developing their art are no longer subject to the frustration of playing an instrument that does not match their skill. The result is that very young musicians are developing incredible facility.

No precision instrument will remain so without the tender loving care of someone who knows how to look after and maintain it. This is not the same skill required to play the instrument, but is as essential to the performance of it. But what about the precision instrument that plays the music. What about the musician? Who maintains the symmetry, balance and coordination of the person who plays? This instrument is not carefully and safely secreted away in a soft lined case to prevent damage but between 'plays' is living the life of everyone else, with the same knocks and life stress, emotional upheaval and daily demand. After only a few years training a very young musician can be entering world class playing, often before they are very well developed themselves.

Most Performance Training Colleges offer The Alexander Technique to provide maintenance for musicians and actors and emphasize how important it is to be aware of the fundamental principles of efficient and effortless movement and function. Direction and inhibition are taught in individual lessons and classes in such a way that performers aim to be able to objectively steer their playing clear of the interferences from mind and body that habitually lessen their performance. This works very well for those that have no fundamental structural problems.

By the term fundamental structural problem I mean a misalignment of the cranium, pelvis, knees, feet or other part of the bone structure that reduces the ability to balance easily and effortlessly on two feet, thereby causing stress to parts of or all of one's function. This misalignment can be caused by or be causing misalignment of the jaw joints (the TMJ) and malocclusion (irregular meeting of the teeth).

In the presence of a misaligned structure the autonomic nervous system, which is designed to protect us and is therefore involuntary, will limit function in spite of will, control, or best efforts. Direction and inhibition cannot override this. As no one is perfectly symmetrical and most of us have some structural deficiencies this is a potentially negative situation, with everyone held back from the development of potential by our autonomic nervous system. However, there is yet another factor to be considered in the balance between player and performance – the desire, the will, the determination, the 'forsaking all other' desire to play music.

This is what I finally came to see was 'the devil within' and although for me, Mick Jagger, Johann Sebastian Bach, Wolfgang Amadeus Mozart or Judy Garland the drive was music, I now see that it could be the desire to paint, to throw the javelin further than anyone else, to sail around the world, dance on ice or to do anything else that requires a high degree of balance, coordination, rhythm and commitment. Whatever it is you want to and can do, choice is somehow removed at a deep primeval level. You have to do it or life is not complete.

It is possible that this desire is as primitive as the evolutionary drive for the fish to make it onto the land, or the bird to develop the wings to fly. The early years from infancy to six years old are a resumé of the stages of evolution, so why should not the primitive desire of 'the moth for the star' be a reflex pattern as inherent in infants as crawling or upright posture.

Technology may satisfy much of the desire for advancement of the species, but it does not cater for the exercise of the emotions or the spirit. Music on the other hand stretches the human physical, intellectual and emotional attributes every way and is available to children through singing.

There will always be those who have good balance, optimal symmetry and a developmental and inspiring childhood. These are the likely high flyers in all skills, including academia. They carry no excess weight, have high energy levels and push themselves very hard because they have lots of adaptive range, not being used up coping with physical or dental distress and not knowing fear or failure. Their skill has been encouraged and nurtured and is not frustrated by the primary instrument – themselves - not functioning as efficiently as it might to produce what is in their creative imagination. They play what they have practiced and programmed. They enjoy the excitement of the devil within and have an efficient and exciting working relationship with it.

But if everyone is born with the devil within, for some it does not survive childhood. Some children who develop serious structural problems of asymmetry that are not detected may never try to push boundaries because their early environment does not stimulate them to do so. The lack of confidence that imbalance and poor development causes may mean that they never do anything that takes them outside their adaptive range. As adults they may not even experience as much as an aching back because they live happily within their adaptation. They may have lacked the stimulation and supportive environment that every child needs to develop personal courage, but it may have saved them from a frustration that would have been impossible to avoid.

For these two groups life's direction can be pretty clear and predictable.

However, there are those with creative skill and the inner desire to push boundaries that is encouraged and nurtured when they are young, who also have simultaneously developing structural problems through minor birth trauma that have never been recognised. The more they develop the less they will be able to cope with the lack of balance and symmetry, which may eventually affect the standard of their performance. But this 'running out of string' can take years, during which there has been a taste of glory. A lower standard is not acceptable. This is where the devil within can become destructive. This doesn't only apply to physical achievement. You are not just a mechanism. Academic skills also suffer in the presence of misalignment. No skill is exempt.

Evidence shows that this group of potential high flyers with structural problems is increasing in numbers with each generation.

Johann Sebastian Bach's grandfather, born in 1613, lived through the worst of the thirty years' war, which began in 1618, in which two thirds of the population in the area we now call Germany were wiped out. The war resulted in mass graves, many of which have been found. In those that have been excavated most of the skeletons still have all of their teeth, including the wisdom teeth. This is the case in most of the excavated skulls up to the period of the Industrial Revolution

Johann Sebastian, the grandson and undisputed father of Western music, was born in 1685, lived and composed prolifically until he was eighty six. He lost his first wife to a mysterious illness, and of his second family of thirteen children only six survived more than a few years. Two died at three years old, one at four and the rest in child birth. This is not an unfamiliar family history, it just happens to be one that is well recorded. It tells us that the infant mortality rate was very high. It then remained so throughout the next two hundred years. It also tells us that if you survived, like Johann Sebastian, you must have had the structural integrity and well developed dentition to cope with the incredibly hard life with no modern facilities, few medical skills and bone-shaking transport. You must also have had a very strong immune system to be surrounded as you were, by stinking open drains, refuse and disease. These conditions were not to dramatically change until the end of the Nineteenth Century. The great achievers of the next two hundred years must have been considerably stronger and fitter than we are today.

Weston Price[1], dentist, went on a world tour in the 1930s to compare the dentition of the so called civilised world with that of peoples still outside of western influence. He discovered that they had almost no dental or jaw problems at all. Later, when he returned after Western influence had

---

[1] Price WA, (2000) *Nutrition & Physical degeneration.* Price-Pottenger Foundation, Lemon Grove CA, ISBN 0-87983-816-7

spread to their community, and particularly when a western diet had infiltrated, faces were narrowing and teeth were crowding and decaying, generation by generation.

The West no longer has a major problem of infant mortality. However, it has other major problems of diet and nutrition, lack of natural exercise and a consumer society, with its questionable values. We have fewer natural births than twenty years ago - more women are opting for caesarean section. We may have more babies survive, but are the ones that do survive structurally weaker? We certainly have many more problems with teeth and jaws than is evident in the skulls of our forefathers. Compared to preceding generations our immune systems are weaker and our physical strength is reduced. If no policy is put in place for checking our developing potential achievers then more and more of them will run out of steam and struggle with frustrated ability.

Parents and teachers need to begin to take the early development of children seriously enough to learn what can be done to assist the process. Babies can be checked after birth by a cranial osteopath or chiropractor for minor birth trauma to prevent the gradual development of major problems when adaptive range is exhausted. We now know what to look for during the early years of a growing, developing child: in teeth, shape of the roof of the mouth, ability to nose breath, balance on two feet and much more. The clinicians who can deal with all this are now in the community. Dentistry is moving towards early assessment at seven or eight years old and preventative treatment. The current policy of orthodontic treatment between ages of thirteen and sixteen limits many high flyers because dental appliances are introduced when skills in sport and music are just maturing

Vocal skills, in both speaking and singing, suffer most from physical and dental misalignment because you are both the player and the instrument. You cannot borrow someone else's instrument to play to identify whether the problem is in the way you are approaching the task, or the instrument itself. You cannot put the instrument away for a couple of days and do something else, or go on holiday to clear your mind. Emotional or physical trauma can put a dent in the instrument, however carefully you protect it. Vocal problems are like toothache. There is no relief except dealing with the cause.

On June 10th 1922 a little girl was born in Grand Rapids, Minnesota. Her mother's pregnancy was inopportune, family plans did not include another baby and her mother could not obtain an abortion, although she did try through a medical friend. She had two or three goes at falling down the stairs but this little girl was going to be born. Forty seven years later the world agonized over the tragic death of one of the 'greatest voices of the Twentieth Century'. Not Callas, not Caruso, but Frances Ethel Gumm, known universally as Judy Garland. After a musically stimulating childhood her ability to present a song was recognised by MGM studios, but they did not like her appearance. She was small, slightly pudgy and had raggedy teeth. She was described by David Shipman[2] in his book *Garland* as 'small, with curvature of the spine. Her legs appeared to begin at her shoulder. Her teeth were uneven and needed to be capped. A little putty gave her a more photogenic nose'. She was also given pills in an attempt to slim her down.

There is no doubt that Judy Garland suffered physical, dental and subsequently emotional and spiritual distress and that she ran out of coping quite early in her life. Her extraordinary talent to move people with her singing is often forgotten in the bad press she had for her drinking, her addiction to drugs and her impossible behaviour. With the right structural and dental help she may not have needed any of it.

---

[2] Shipman, D. (1993) Judy Garland. Harper Collins, London, ISBN 0-00-637961-3.

Also by Angela Caine

Early VoiceGym

Early VoiceGym is a simple Voice and Body Exercise programme for children from 5 to 10 years old to develop singing, speech and posture. This will provide an invaluable tool to any parent, teacher or music therapy specialist. It does not just encourage singing and movement of children, and leave you 'hands free' to move and sing with them, but explains the links between the development of the voice and the development of posture, coordination and dentition (not generally covered in music teacher training), and how these can effect the voice.

The aims of Early VoiceGym are -

- To get children singing well at an early age;
- To give children better speech to read aloud and communicate with;
- To reinforce early stages in the development of posture, coordination, dentition and intelligence;
- To inform parents an teachers how to bring this about and give them the tools to do.

The complete Early VoiceGym pack includes -

- Early VoiceGym SongBook - a book with exercises and songs with instructions and an audio CD;
- Early VoiceGym NoteBook - a book of notes on the early development of children and the background to the exercises;
- A DVD demonstrating the programme with children;
- Two stretch bands of different weights - one light for children, one medium for an adult.

ISBN 978-0-9553799-3-2

Available from www.voicegym.co.uk

Also by Angela Caine

VoiceGym

VoiceGym gives you all the fundamental exercise materials and other essential tools that Angela Caine uses for voice work in singing or speech with teenagers and adults. The exercises are all very simple and are explained clearly and with photographs. You can improve your voice by yourself with this system if you follow the simple instructions and practice regularly.

The VoiceGym Pack contains -

- An A4 book of exercises with instructions, poems and songs in a large clear font;
- An audio CD of exercises, songs and backing tracks, with male and female voices;
- A physio-ball for balance, rhythm and stretch;
- A stretch band for whole body stretch and rotation: upper body repositioning and balance;
- A toothbrush ("A toothbrush?" - "Yes, a toothbrush");
- A wooden balance board for back strengthening, posture and extending pitch range;
- An animal beanbag for work on posture and singing (and fun);
- VoiceGym Book - *Get to Know your Voice* - the text book that explains it all (see next page).

ISBN 978-0-9553799-5-6

Also by Angela Caine

VoiceGym Book - get to know your voice

VoiceGym Book contains the background, teaching experience and research, sometimes in disciplines not previously related to voice, that has created *VoiceGym*.

This book updates information on important issues like tongue position, breathing, the function of face muscles, how to maintain their efficient function, and how to manage a voice for life.

Simple diagrams, models and photographs make clear the interaction between brain, body and voice. The multidisciplinary approach will help you to think out of the box and question received wisdom when this is not supplying the answers that you need.

- A book for the development and understanding of voice in the 21st Century.

- A book to bring together all the fragmented information related to voice and explain how it all interacts to give efficient speech and singing to everyone.

- A book to explain to singers, actors, teachers and other professional voice users the links between functional anatomy, dentistry and skeletal misalignment.

ISBN 978-0-9553799-0-1